60 Hikes Within 60 Miles: RALEIGH

60 Hikes Within 60 Miles:

RALEIGH

LYNN SETZER

1st Edition

MENASHA RIDGE PRESS
Birmingham, Alabama

To Rob Levin who, a long time ago, told
me to start "local."

Copyright © 2001 Lynn Setzer
All rights reserved
Manufactured in the United States of America
Published by Menasha Ridge Press
Distributed by The Globe Pequot Press
First edition, first printing

Library of Congress Cataloging-in-Publication Data

Setzer, Lynn, 1955-
  60 hikes in 60 miles, Raleigh/by Lynn Setzer
  p. cm.
  Includes index
  ISBN 0-89732-332-7 (alk. paper)
  1. Hiking—North Carolina—Raleigh Region—Guidebooks. 2. Raleigh Region
(N.C.)—Guidebooks. I. Title: Sixty hikes within sixty miles, Raleigh. II. Title
GV199.42.N662 R257 2001
796,51'09756'55—dc21

                                                              00-068365
                                                                   CIP

Cover and text design by Grant M. Tatum
Maps by Susanna Fillingham and Steve Jones
Cover photo by Dennis Coello
All other photos by Lynn Setzer

Menasha Ridge Press
P.O. Box 43673
Birmingham, AL 35243
www.menasharidge.com

Table of Contents

Table of Contents (continued)

——————— Main Trail

▪▪▪▪▪▪▪▪▪▪▪ Alternate Trail

Interstate Highway

US Highway

State Highway

County Road

Forest Service Road

Local Road

Unpaved Road

Direction of Travel

State Border

County Border

NATIONAL OR STATE FOREST/PARK

Park–Forest Boundary and Label

Trailhead Locator Map

Lake Blue
Blue River

Water Features
Lake/Pond, Creek/River, and Waterfall

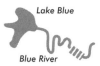
CAPITOL   TOWN
        CITY

capitol, city, and town

Mt. Maggie
3,312'

Peaks and Mountains

)( )((
Footbridge/Dam, Footbridge, and Dam

◗◖
Tunnel

Swamp/Marsh

NORTH

35: Name of Hike

Map Scale

Compass, Map Number, Name and Scale

◀
Off map or pinpoint indication arrow

Trailhead for specific Maps

Ranger Station/ Rest Room Facilities

Ranger Station

Rest Room Facilities

Shelter

Structure or Feature

Monument/ Sculpture

P
Parking

R
Recreation Area

Campgrounds

Picnic Area

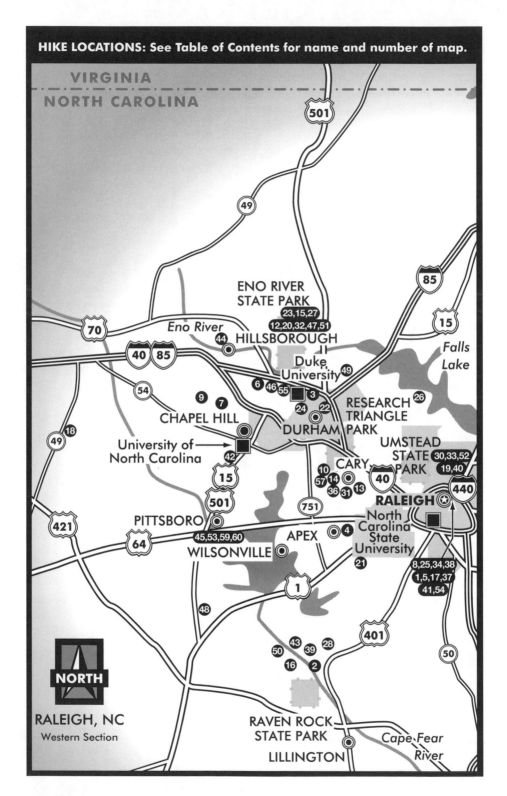

HIKE LOCATIONS: See Table of Contents for name and number of map.

VIRGINIA
NORTH CAROLINA

501

49

85

70

ENO RIVER
STATE PARK
23,15,27
12,20,32,47,51

15

40 85

Eno River
44 HILLSBOROUGH

Falls
Lake

Duke
University 49

54

6 46 55 3

RESEARCH
TRIANGLE
PARK

26

9 7

CHAPEL HILL

24 22

49 18

University of
North Carolina

DURHAM

UMSTEAD
STATE
PARK

30,33,52
19,40

42

10
57 14
36 31

CARY

40

15

501

751

13

440

RALEIGH ★

PITTSBORO

64

45,53,59,60

APEX

North
Carolina
State
University

421

WILSONVILLE

4

8,25,34,38
1,5,17,37
41,54

21

1

48

401

NORTH

43 39

28

50

RALEIGH, NC
Western Section

50 39

16 2

RAVEN ROCK
STATE PARK

LILLINGTON

Cape Fear
River

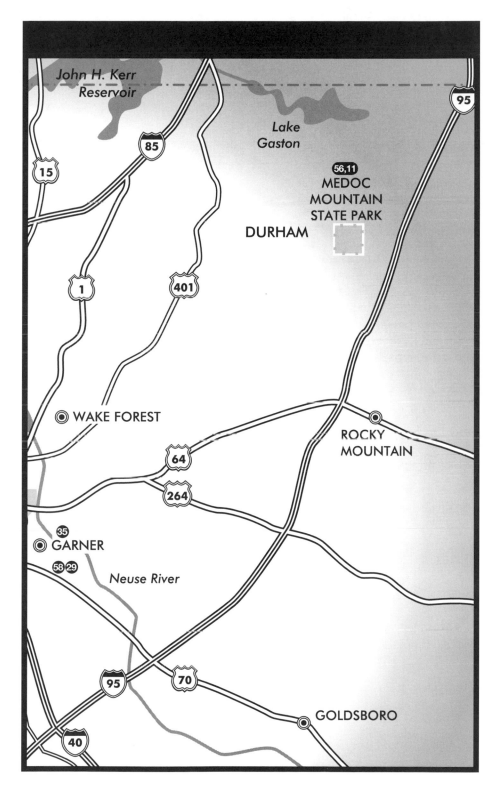

Acknowledgments

Without help from the following people, this book would not have come together. I am indebted—and extend a heartfelt thanks—to:

• Bud Zehmer, who, in offering this wonderful project to me, helped me find yet another reason to take a hike.

• Russell Helms, my editor at Menasha Ridge Press, who held steady when I asked off-the-wall questions or panicked.

• Randall Washington, who hiked the majority of these trails with me, in good weather and bad. Didn't we have some fun in the winter with the cold winds and near-zero temps and in the summer with the cobwebs and copperheads? You really are a good sport!

• Ellen Benzine, Thresa Pressley, Mary Ann Flournoy, Tracie Thomas, and Jack Mixell, who all found a little time in their busy lives to hike with me.

• All of the park rangers in the state, city, and county parks who answered questions for me, but especially the staff at Eno River State Park. They let me plunder many files, gleaning historical information about the area.

Foreword

Welcome to Menasha Ridge Press's *60 Hikes Within 60 Miles,* a series designed to provide hikers with the information to find and hike the very best trails surrounding U.S. cities such as Raleigh, which are usually under-served by thorough guidebooks.

Our goal was simple: First, find a hiker who knows the area and loves to hike. Second, ask that person to spend a year researching the most popular and the very best trails around. And third, have that person describe each trail in terms of difficulty, scenery, condition, elevation change, and other categories of information that are important to hikers.

"Pretend you've just completed a hike and met up with other hikers at the trailhead," we told each author. "Imagine their questions. Be clear in your answers."

With a wealth of green forests, coastal plains, and ancient mountains, North Carolina is within driving distance of nearly two-thirds of the United States population. So before you Raleigh-area residents and visitors go off to hike the Appalachian Trail or climb Everest, why not get to know your own backyard first?

An experienced hiker and writer, author Lynn Setzer has selected 60 of her favorite hikes in and around her hometown of Raleigh. From the civilized greenways of Raleigh and Cary to the rugged trails of Raven Rock State Park, Setzer provides hikers (and walkers) with a great variety of trails—all within 60 miles of Raleigh.

You'll get more out of this book if you take a moment to read the Introduction explaining how to read the trail listings. The "Topographic Maps" section will help you understand how useful topos are on a hike, and will also tell you where to get them. And though this is a "where-to," not a "how-to" guide, those of you who have not hiked extensively will find the Introduction of particular value.

As much for the opportunity to liberate your legs as to limber your mind, let Setzer's hikes elevate you above the urban hurry.

All the best.
The editors at Menasha Ridge Press

Preface

One of the many things I discovered while exploring these hikes and pulling this book together is that the increasingly urban Triangle, contrary to my previous notions, has many top-notch trails to hike.

I admit I was skeptical when I first took on this project. I wasn't sure the area would have enough quality trails to include (in fact, this book doesn't list all of the area's trails). I like a trail where I can leave the desk-jockey world behind, if only for a while. Plus, I'm a long-distance-view snob. I don't mind a steep hike if there's some sort of soul-expanding vista to "oooh" and "ahhh" over when I get there.

What I found is that what this area lacks in outstanding, knock 'em dead views, it makes up for in historic walks and reclaimed forests. And, there are more wildflowers that bloom here than I realized. Finally, I also discovered that we do have a pocketful of knock 'em dead views. Not many, of course, because this side of the Piedmont slopes down to the North Carolina coastal plain, but enough to do the trick.

I also found that those of us who live here get out and enjoy our trails. Weekends, particularly in the spring and fall, are busy. During the winter, however, crowds

Stop by Cedarock Park and visit this cabin built in 1835.

subside; if you're looking for less busy trails, you'll certainly find them in the winter! There's absolutely no reason to sit inside dying of boredom just because there's a little chill to the air.

I also discovered that, during the summer, Triangle trails have an abundance—an overabundance in some places—of poison ivy. If you're going to hike in the summer, learn to recognize this weed so that you can steer very clear of it. I was very fortunate not to catch any of the stuff until the last hike I took.

About the Major Parks

In picking these hikes, I focused on the four state parks in the area: Umstead, Eno River, Raven Rock and Medoc Mountain. In addition, I visited two incredible city parks: Cary's Bond Park and Durham's West Point on the Eno. I also spent some time on the greenways, as well as at Jordan Lake, a state recreation area. Although the hike descriptions give you an indication of what you're likely to see along a particular trail, each park deserves a little more explanation.

Eno River State Park

My favorite state park! My first visit occurred six years ago in early November, when just enough leaves had fallen that I could really see the steep walls cut by the Eno, but before the trees were completely bare. I had not hiked more than ten minutes along the Cox Mountain trail before I understood why Margaret Nygard had fought so hard for the Eno.

If you haven't heard Nygard's story, it bears repeating. In 1965, the town of Durham floated an idea to dam the Eno River in order to create a reservoir; the town needed the water. Durham citizen Margaret Nygard led a core group of protestors, which came to be known as the Eno River Association, to stop that idea from becoming a reality. Too much history, in the form of eighteenth century river

fords and roadbeds, and nineteenth century gristmills, would be put under water, she argued. Opportunities to explore archaeological remnants of the Eno, Shakori, and Occoneechee tribes that lived in the area prior to the arrival of Europeans would be lost. More than that, the beauty of the river valley itself would be destroyed.

The Eno River Association, led by Nygard, worked hard to save the river. An annual Fourth of July event, Festival for the Eno, began as a fund-raiser to enable the Association to acquire lands surrounding the river. With help from the state and the Nature Conservancy, the area became a state park in 1975. Today, thousands of people turn out each year for Festival for the Eno to support the Eno River Association's conservancy efforts.

As rivers go, the Eno isn't particularly long, only about 20 miles. There was a time when the surrounding land was laid bare by timber companies. Today, however, when you hike here, you can marvel at the boulder-strewn river and enjoy a sense of remoteness unheard of anywhere else in the Triangle.

The recovering forest contains lots of hickories, oaks, sweet gums, sycamores, red maples, and dogwoods. Though you probably won't see any beavers, you certainly will see evidence of their presence, such as gnawed trees. You should also see herons.

Park information indicates that fishing along the Eno is good. I've never wet a hook there, but those who do catch largemouth bass, Roanoke bass, bluegill, chain pickerel, and crappie. Of course, you must have a valid NC fishing license.

Paddlers, too, are fond of the Eno, particularly in the spring when the river runs high. Rapids are rated Class I, II, and III.

As for me, I prefer hiking there in the winter, because that's when I can really see the river. That first November hike was absolutely perfect.

If you are interested in becoming an Eno River activist or if you want to join the outings they sponsor, contact the Eno River Association at 4419 Guess Road, Durham, NC 27712; at (919) 620-9099; or at www.enoriver.org.

The park is open daily, with seasonal hours, except for Christmas and New Year's Days. The park's phone number is (919) 383-1686.

Clemmons Educational State Forest

In recent years hurricanes have hit this state forest hard as they roared through. Nonetheless, it still does an admirable job working with local educators in offering programs to school kids.

The forest is open mid-March through mid-November. Hours are Tuesday–Friday, 9 a.m.–5 p.m.; Saturday and Sunday, 11 a.m.–5 p.m. The forest is closed on Mondays. They can be reached at (919) 553-5651.

Fred G. Bond Metro Park and Cary Greenways

The Town of Cary did a fabulous day's work when it set aside 570 acres for Bond Park, the largest municipal park in Wake County. I was surprised, frankly, to find a park this large and this attractive in a town known for rapid development. The 42-acre lake is open to fishing and boating (remember to have that fishing license). If you don't have a boat, you can rent pedal boats, rowboats, canoes, and sailboats, as well as electric motors for rowboats.

This park is also busy with youth ropes courses and orienteering programs, plus it has a number of ballfields.

If you have a Frisbee-catching dog, you might want to enter one of the Canine Frisbee competitions.

Bond Park is open daily with seasonal hours, and their phone number is (919) 469-4100.

Currently, Cary's greenways are a little on the short side, but this shouldn't last

forever. According to development plans, Cary soon will have many more long-distance greenway trails.

Jordan Lake State Recreation Area

My earliest memory of Jordan Lake comes from the days before the lake was filled with water.

Traveling west on US 64, I'd ride over the Jordan Lake bridge and see the network of roads being used by heavy-duty earth-moving equipment. The landscape was so barren it reminded me of a moonscape. Then, one day, the lake filled with water and the moonscape became a bona fide lake and reservoir for the growing Triangle area.

Until recently, I was unaware of the circumstances that motivated the state and the Army Corps of Engineers to create Jordan Lake. In 1945 a hurricane—imagine that, a hurricane!—struck the Cape Fear River basin. So great was the damage to fresh water resources that Congress directed the Army Corps of Engineers to study and plan for the water requirements of the area. As a result, in 1963, the New Hope Lake project began.

The New Hope River Valley, as the area was once known, provided food and shelter to Native Americans for more than 10,000 years. Archaeologists have discovered the remains of 450 prehistoric and historic sites. As in the area to the south of Wake County, Scots Highlanders settled here in the mid-1700s.

Today, the 46,768-acre lake is a busy spot for boating, swimming, kayaking, cycling, eagle-watching, and hiking. I can vouch personally for sunset kayaking and cycling. The water of Jordan Lake glows a marvelous pink at sunset, and the roads are, for the area, surprisingly flat. On many Saturday mornings my husband and I have parked our car in the lot of one of the country churches, assumed a riding position and gone for a spin on our bikes. Nor are

Crabtree Creek, along the Company Mill Trail in Umstead State Park.

we alone in pedaling here; NC 751 is busy with bicycles on weekend mornings.

In addition to all of these activities, there are hiking trails. Short and easy, these trails weave in and around the area, making good hikes for short legs.

Jordan Lake is open daily; the office can be reached at (919) 362-0586.

Medoc Mountain State Park

Curiosity drove my discovery of Medoc Mountain. I was looking for a different place to take a hike—one where there was a chance for solitude—plus I was curious about a state park this far east calling itself a mountain. Moreover, I was curious about the name. In an area loaded with English- and Scottish-derived names, a French name, reminiscent of wine-making country, is unusual.

Well, there is a mountain here, but you won't have commanding views from the top. You'll know it's a mountain, though, because the ascending trail isn't exactly easy! You'll huff and puff a bit to get on top.

When you depart the park to return home, you'll have a glimpse from the road of how high you are. Drive slowly from the park entrance, not more than 0.2 mile, to see this view.

The mountain was named by Sidney Weller, a noted farmer and educator who lived here in the mid-1800s. Renowned for his help in producing the first North Carolina State Fair in 1853, Weller also is known for producing a highly acclaimed wine—Weller's Halifax—and is credited by some with starting the American system of grape culture.

After Weller's death in 1854, the property changed hands several times, was farmed, and then timbered.

In the 1940s, when molybdenum was discovered, it looked as if the area might be mined. Fortunately, in 1975, the area became a park.

The Carolina mudpuppy, a rather large aquatic salamander, has been spotted in Little Fishing Creek, the creek that splits the park into two halves. I haven't seen the

One of several stone bridges crossing Sycamore Creek in Umstead State Park.

scarce mudpuppy myself, though I did watch a turtle munch through a mushroom, a different kind of rare sighting. If you grew up listening to bobwhites call each other, you will appreciate hearing them here.

The park is open daily, with seasonal hours, except for Christmas and New Year's Days. Call (252) 586-6588 for more information.

Raleigh Greenways

In discussing with Bud Zehmer, at Menasha Ridge Press, which hikes to include in this book, I was amused when he asked the same question I had asked of myself earlier.

"Aren't you putting too many greenway paths in there?"

The more I hiked, though, the more I realized just how good the Raleigh Greenway system is. This books lists about a third of those trails.

In 1974, Raleigh took action to design a master plan for its greenway system. Now,

over 25 years later, the city is closing in on its plan to have a 27.5-mile system of connected trails. All of the folks, both past and present, who have worked hard to make the Raleigh Greenway system what it is today, deserve a round of applause.

The best map for scoping out the greenways is the Raleigh Bike Map, published by the NCDOT Bicycle Program. On this map, you can see city parks and bike routes as well as the greenways.

Raven Rock State Park

Another environmental jewel, Raven Rock State Park should be celebrated more than it is. Trust me, you haven't seen a rock until you view massive Raven Rock as it juts out over the Cape Fear River.

My first hike here, on a January day some eight years ago, was simply great. It destroyed my wrong-headed notion that there were no spectacular views in this area of the North Carolina Piedmont. The Campbell Creek/Lanier Falls excursion was just the right amount of distance and the scenery of Lanier Falls and of the Cape Fear River well worth the effort. Then, just when I thought I couldn't be any more impressed, I saw the view from the Raven Rock balcony.

My only regret about hiking here is that I've yet to see the mountain laurel in bloom. My friend Tracie makes hiking here in the spring an annual pilgrimage just to be able to see it.

If you're a paddler, Raven Rock State Park holds additional charms: six campsites especially for canoeists. Sites include tent pads, fire circles, and an outhouse. You can contact the park office at (910) 893-4888 to reserve a site.

Fishing is permitted during park hours. The Fish Traps Trail and Campbell Creek/Lanier Falls Trail are the best places to wet a hook.

The park is open daily, with seasonal hours, except for Christmas and New Year's Days. Call the park at (910) 893-4888 for more information.

Umstead State Park

Last, but certainly not least, is Umstead State Park. This 5000-plus-acre park, called Central Park by those who fear the rapidly growing Triangle is about to swallow the park on all sides, can't be beaten as a place to go outside and play. No matter when you go, no matter which side you visit, you're sure to see people in this park biking, hiking, fishing, running, or picnicking.

As you walk through the woods here, try to imagine what the area looked like when it was farmland. In fact, the land was so overfarmed, that, by the 1930s, the soil was seriously depleted, as well as eroded. In 1934, the federal government stepped in to buy the land, restore, and then develop it as a recreation area. Later, after the federal government finished its work, the state bought the park for $1.00. I think that dollar is one of the single best dollars the state has ever spent.

Three man-made lakes are open to fishing; bridle trails are open to bikers; and equestrian courses, picnic shelters and group camping facilities are open to all who want to use them. At night, the woods are alive with the sound of owls hootie-hooing away. I took my first hike here some 20 years ago, and I count myself among the frequent visitors.

Like Eno River State Park, Umstead has a watchdog and educational organization to call its own: the Umstead Coalition. They can be contacted at Umstead Coalition, Box 10654, Raleigh, NC 27605. The Coalition's phone number is (919) 852-2268. Or, check out their Web site at www.umsteadcoalition.org.

The park is open daily, with seasonal hours, except for Christmas and New Year's Days. To contact the park call (919) 571-4170.

Hiking Recommendations

Hikes under 1 Mile
American Beech Trail
Crowder District Park Trails
Fallon Creek Trail
Shepherd Nature Trail
Talking Trees Trail

Hikes from 1 to 3 Miles
Apex Reservoir Greenway
Art Museum Trail
Beaver Dam/Hymettus Woods
Bond Fitness Trail
Buckquarter Creek Trail
Cedarock Nature Trails Combo
Duke Cross–Country Trail
Durham Pump Station
Old Ebenezer Church
Fanny's Ford
Fish Traps Trail
Frances L. Liles Trail
Hemlock Bluffs
Inspiration Trail
Ironwood Ramble
Lake Benson Trail
Lake Lynn Trail
Little Creek Trail
Big Oak Woods Trail
North Carolina Botanical Garden
Northington Ferry
Occoneechee Mountain
Penny's Bend Ridge and River Hike
Raven Rock Loop
Seaforth Trail
Symphony Lake
Vista Point Recreation Area
Wildlife Observation Trail

Hikes from 3 to 6 Miles
Alleghany Ramble
Black Creek Greenway/Lake Trail
Bluff Loop/Stream Loop
Bobbitt's Hole/Cole Mill
Campbell Creek with Lanier Falls Spur
Camp Durant Ramble
Cox Mountain Trail
Dam Site Summit Loop
Eno River, North and South
Forest Demonstration
Lake Crabtree Trail
Lake Johnson Trail
Old Oxford Road
Pea Creek/Dunnagan's Ramble
Peninsula Trail
Ridge Trail/Shakori Ramble
Sal's Branch/Pott's Branch

Hikes over 6 Miles
American Tobacco Trail
Battle Branch/Bolin Creek Ramble
Bond Lake Loop
Company Mill Trail
Falls Lake Trail
Loblolly Trail
Neuse River Trail

Hikes Good for Young Children
American Beech Trail
Apex Reservoir Greenway
Bond Fitness Trail
Crowder District Park
Fallon Creek Trail
Lake Lynn Greenway
Little Creek Trail

Seaforth Trail
Shepherd Nature Trail
Talking Trees Trail

Urban Hikes
Alleghany Ramble
American Tobacco Trail
Art Museum Trail
Battle Branch/Bolin Creek Ramble
Beaver Dam/Hymettus Woods
Eno River Trail, North and South
Fallon Creek Trail
Ironwood Ramble
Lake Johnson Trail
Lake Lynn Greenway
Shelley Lake Loop with Bent Creek

Hikes with Steep Sections
Battle Branch/Bolin Creek Ramble
Company Mill Trail
Cox Mountain Trail
Summit Trail/Dam Site Combo
Duke Cross–Country Trail
Fish Traps Trail
Hemlock Bluffs Ramble
North Carolina Botanical Garden
Northington Ferry
Occoneechee Mountain
Raven Rock Loop
Ridge Trail/Shakori Ramble

Lake Hikes
Apex Reservoir Greenway
Old Ebenezer Church
Lake Benson Trail
Lake Crabtree Trail
Lake Johnson Trail
Lake Lynn Greenway
Peninsula Trail
Seaforth Trail
Symphony Lake
Vista Point Recreation Area
Wildlife Observation Trail

Scenic Hikes
Bobbitt's Hole/Cole Mill Trail

Buckquarter Creek Trail
Fallon Creek Trail
Hemlock Bluffs Ramble
Occoneechee Mountain
Raven's Rock Loop
Bluff Loop/Stream Loop

Historic Hikes
American Tobacco Trail
Buckquarter Creek Trail
Durham Pump Station
Fanny's Ford
Cedarock Nature Trails Combo
Holden's Mill Trail
Northington Ferry
Pea Creek/Dunnagan's Ramble

Hikes for Wildlife Viewing
Buckquarter Creek Trail
Bluff Loop/Stream Loop
Holden's Mill Trail
Big Oak Woods Trail
Sal's Branch/Pott's Branch

Hikes for Wildflowers
Bald Mountain Trail
Black Creek Greenway/Lake Trail
Penny's Bend Ridge and River Hike
Hemlock Bluffs Ramble
North Carolina Botanical Garden
Cedarock Nature Trails Combo

Hikes Demonstrating Forest Management Practices
Talking Trees Trail
Frances L. Liles Trail
Forest Demonstration Trail
Loblolly Trail
Shepherd Nature Trail

Trails for Runners
Alleghany Ramble
American Tobacco Trail
Apex Reservoir Greenway
Art Museum Trail
Black Creek Greenway/Lake Trail

Bond Fitness Trail
Fallon Creek Trail
Crowder District Park
Duke Cross–Country Trail
Lake Benson Trail
Lake Johnson Trail
Lake Lynn Greenway
Shelley Lake Loop with Bent Creek
Symphony Lake

Trails for Cyclists
Alleghany Ramble
American Tobacco Trail
Apex Reservoir Greenway
Art Museum Trail
Bald Mountain Trail
Black Creek Greenway/Lake Trail
Fallon Creek Trail
Crowder District Park
Duke Cross–Country Trail
Lake Benson Trail
Lake Johnson Trail
Lake Lynn Greenway
Old Oxford Road
Shelley Lake Loop with Bent Creek
Symphony Lake

Less Busy Hikes
Bald Mountain Trail
Bluff Loop/Stream Loop
Summit Trail/Dam Site Combo
Durham Pump Station
Old Ebenezer Church
Big Oak Woods Trail
Occoneechee Mountain Trail
Peninsula Trail
Penny's Bend Ridge and River Hike
Ridge Trail/Shakori Ramble

Heavily Traveled Hikes
American Beech Trail
American Tobacco Trail
Apex Reservoir Greenway
Duke Cross–Country Trail
Frances L. Liles Trail
Lake Benson Trail
Lake Johnson Trail
Lake Lynn Greenway
North Carolina Botanical Garden
Shelley Lake Loop with Bent Creek
Raven Rock Loop
All hikes in Umstead State Park

Introduction

Welcome to *60 Hikes within 60 Miles: Raleigh!* If you're new to hiking or even if you're a seasoned trail-smith, take a few minutes to read the following introduction. We'll explain how this book is organized and how to use it.

Hike Profiles

Each hike contains six key items: a locator map, an In Brief description of the trail, an At-a-Glance Information box, directions to the trail, a trail map, and a hike narrative. Combined, the maps and information provide a clear method for assessing each trail from the comfort of your favorite chair.

Locator Map

After narrowing down the general area of the hike on the overview map (see pages *viii–ix*), the locator map, along with driving directions given in the narrative, enables you to find the trailhead. Once at the trailhead, park only in designated areas.

In Brief

This synopsis of the trail offers a snapshot of what to expect along the trail, including mention of any historical sights, beautiful vistas, or other interesting sights you may encounter.

At-a-Glance Information

The At-a-Glance information boxes give you a quick idea of the specifics of each hike. There are 11 basic elements covered:

Length—The length of the trail from start to finish. There may be options to shorten or extend the hikes, but the mileage corresponds to the described hike. Consult the hike description to help decide how to customize the hike for your ability or time constraints.

Configuration—A description of what the trail might look like from above. Trails can be loops, out-and-backs (hiking in, then retracing your steps), figure eights, or balloons. Sometimes the descriptions might surprise you.

Difficulty—The degree of effort an "average" hiker should expect on a given hike. For simplicity, difficulty is described as easy, moderate, or difficult.

Scenery—Rates the overall environs of the hike and describes what to expect in terms of plant life, wildlife, streams, and historic buildings.

Exposure—A quick check of how much sun you can expect on your shoulders during the hike. Descriptors used are self-explanatory and include terms such as shady, exposed, and sunny.

Solitude—Indicates how busy the trail might be on an average day. Trail traffic, of course, will vary from day to day and season to season.

Trail Surface—Indicates whether the trail is paved, rocky, smooth dirt, or a mixture of surfaces.

Hiking Time—How long it took the author to hike the trail. She admits that she is a fast hiker, except when it comes to hills, where she slows down. Her hiking times include the occasional stop to "smell the roses" or to take in a nice view.

Access—Notes fees or permits required to access the trail. In most cases no fees or permits are required. Always check if in doubt.

Maps—Which map is the best, in the author's opinion, for this hike and where you can get it.

Facilities—Notes any facilities such as rest rooms, phones, and water available at the trailhead or on the trail.

Special Comments—Provides you with those little extra details that don't fit into any of the above categories. Here you'll find information on trail hiking options and facts such as whether or not to expect a lifeguard at a nearby swimming beach.

Directions

Check here for directions to the trailhead. Used with the locator map, the directions will help you locate each trailhead.

Descriptions

The trail description is the heart of each hike. Here, the author provides a summary of the trail's essence as well as any special traits the hike offers. Ultimately, the hike description will help you choose which hikes are best for you.

Nearby Activities

Not every hike will have this listing. For those that do, look here for information on nearby dining opportunities or other activities to fill out your day.

Weather

Fall, winter, and spring are the best seasons to hike in the Triangle area. After mid-October, temperatures tend to moderate. In November and December, you can enjoy the spectacular color of the trees, though after a hard rainstorm or two the trees will be bare. January and February can often be pleasant months to hike in, and if you hike in March and April, you're likely to see lots of jonquils blooming. The flowers remain from the days when much

of the acreage that now comprises our state parks was private farmland. In May and June, when the temperatures begin to soar, you may find that hiking is best done in the early morning or late afternoon.

Average Daily Temperatures (Fahrenheit)
by Month: Raleigh, North Carolina

Jan	Feb	Mar	Apr
38.9	42.0	50.4	59.0
May	**Jun**	**Jul**	**Aug**
67.0	74.3	78.1	77.1
Sep	**Oct**	**Nov**	**Dec**
71.1	60.1	51.2	42.6

Maps

The maps in this book have been produced with great care and, used with the hiking directions, will help you stay on course. But as any experienced hiker knows, things can get tricky off the beaten path.

The maps and route directions in each chapter are sufficient to get you to the trail and keep you on it. However, you will find superior detail and valuable information in the United States Geological Survey's 7.5 minute series topographic maps. Recognizing how indispensable these are to hikers and bikers alike, many outdoor shops and bike shops now carry topos of the local area.

If you're new to hiking you might be wondering, "What's a topographic map?" In short, topos differ from standard "flat" maps; they indicate not only linear distance but elevation as well. One glance at a topo will show you the difference: Contour lines spread across the map like dozens of intricate spider webs. Each contour line represents a particular elevation, and at the base of each topo a contour's interval designation is given. It may sound confusing if you're new to the lingo, but it's truly a simple and helpful system.

Assume that the 7.5 minute series topo reads "Contour Interval 40 feet," that the short trail you'll be hiking is two inches in length on the map, and that it crosses five contour lines from beginning to end. Because the linear scale of this series is 2,000 feet to the inch (roughly two and three-quarters inches representing one mile), the trail is approximately four-fifths of a mile long (2 inches equal 2,000 feet). You'll also be climbing or descending 200 vertical feet (5 contour lines are 40 feet each) over that distance. The elevation designations written on occasional contour lines will tell you if you're heading up or down.

In addition to outdoor shops and bike shops, you'll find topos at major universities and some public libraries, where you might try photocopying the ones you need to avoid the cost of buying them. But if you want your own and can't find them locally, contact USGS Map Sales at Box 25286, Denver, CO 80225; (888) ASK-USGS (275-8747); or www.mapping.usgs.gov.

Visa and MasterCard are accepted. Ask for an index while you're at it, plus a price list and a copy of the booklet *Topographic Maps*. In minutes you'll be reading topos like a pro.

A second excellent series of maps available to hikers is produced by the United States Forest Service. If your trail runs through an area designated as a national forest, look in the phone book (blue pages) for United States Government, find the Department of Agriculture, and run your finger down that section until you locate the Forest Service. Give them a call, and they'll provide the address of the regional Forest Service office, from which you can obtain the appropriate map.

Trail Etiquette

Whether you're on a Cary greenway or on a long hike in Umstead State Park, always remember that great care and resources (from Nature as well as from your tax dollars) went into creating these trails. Taking care of the trails begins with you, the hiker. Treat the trail, wildlife, and fellow hikers with respect. Here are a few general ideas to keep in mind while on the trail.

1. Hike on open trails only. Respect trail and road closures (ask if you're not sure), avoid possible trespass on private land, and obtain all permits and authorization as required. Also, leave gates as you found them or as marked.

2. Leave no trace of your visit other than footprints. Be sensitive to the dirt beneath you. This also means staying on the trail and not creating any new ones. Be sure to pack out what you pack in. No one likes to see trash someone else left behind.

3. Never spook animals. An unannounced approach, a sudden movement, or a loud noise startles most animals. A surprised snake or skunk can be dangerous to you, others, and themselves. Give animals extra room and time to adjust to your presence.

4. Plan ahead. Know your equipment, your ability, and the area in which you are hiking—and prepare accordingly. Be self-sufficient at all times; carry necessary supplies for changes in weather or other conditions. A well-executed trip is a satisfaction to you and not a burden or offense to others.

5. Be courteous to other hikers, or bikers, you meet on the trails.

Water

"How much is enough? One bottle? Two? Three?! But think of all that extra weight!"

Well, one simple physiological fact should convince you to err on the side of excess when it comes to deciding how much water to pack: A human working hard in 90-degree heat needs approximately ten quarts of fluid every day. That's two and a half gallons—12 large water bottles or 16 small ones. And, with water weighing in at approximately 8 pounds per gallon, a one-day supply comes to a whopping 20 pounds.

In other words, pack along one or two bottles even for short hikes. And, make sure you can purify the water found along the trail on longer routes. Drink it untreated, though, and you run the risk of disease.

Many hikers pack along the inexpensive and only slightly distasteful tetraglycine hydroperiodide tablets (sold under the names Potable Aqua, Globaline, and Coughlan's, among others). Some invest in portable, lightweight purifiers that filter out crud. Unfortunately, both iodine and filtering are required to be absolutely sure you've killed all the nasties you can't see.

Tablets or iodine drops by themselves will knock off the well-known Giardia. One to four weeks after ingestion, giardiasis will have you bloated, vomiting, shivering with chills, and living in the bathroom.

But there are other parasites to worry about, including cryptosporidium. "Crypto" brings on symptoms very similar to Giardia, but unlike that fellow protozoan it's equipped with a shell sufficiently strong to protect it against the chemical killers that stop Giardia cold. This means either boiling the water or using a water filter to screen out both Giardia and Crypto, plus the iodine to knock off viruses.

Some water filters come equipped with an iodine chamber to guarantee broad-spectrum protection. Or you can simply add a pill or drops to the water you've just filtered (if you aren't allergic to iodine, of course). The pleasures of hiking—and the displeasure of getting sick—make this relatively minor effort worth every one of the few minutes involved.

First-Aid Kit

A typical kit may contain more items than you might think necessary. These are just the basics:

Sunscreen
Aspirin or acetaminophen

Butterfly-closure bandages
Band-Aids
Snakebite kit
Gauze (one roll)
Gauze compress pads (a half-dozen 4 in. x 4 in.)
Ace bandages or Spenco joint wraps
Benadryl or the generic equivalent— diphenhydramine (an antihistamine, in case of allergic reactions)
A prefilled syringe of epinephrine (for those known to have severe allergic reactions to such things as bee stings)
Water purification tablets or water filter (on longer hikes)
Moleskin/Spenco "Second Skin"
Hydrogen peroxide or iodine
Antibiotic ointment (Neosporin or the generic equivalent)
Matches or pocket lighter
Whistle (more effective in signaling rescuers than your voice)

Pack the items in a waterproof container such as a Ziploc bag or a similar product.

Hiking with Children

No one is ever too young for a nice hike in the woods or through a city park. Parents with infants can strap the little ones on with the popular Snuggly device. Be careful, though.

Flat, short trails are probably best with an infant. Toddlers who have not quite mastered walking can still tag along, riding on an adult's back in a child carrier.

Children who are walking can, of course, follow along slowly with an adult. Use common sense to judge a child's capacity to hike a particular trail, and always rely on the possibility that the child will tire quickly and have to be carried.

When packing for the hike, remember the needs of the child as well as your own. Make sure children are adequately clothed for the weather, have proper shoes, and are properly protected from the sun with sunscreen and clothing. Kids dehydrate quickly, so make sure you have plenty of fluid for everyone.

Depending on their age, ability, and the hike's difficulty, most children should enjoy the shorter hikes described in this book. To assist adults in determining which trails are suitable for children, a list of hike recommendations for children is provided on page *xx*.

The Business Hiker

Whether doing business in the Triangle area as a resident or visitor, these 60 hikes are the perfect opportunity to make a quick get-away from the demands of commerce. Many of the hikes are classified as urban and are easily accessible from downtown areas.

Instead of a burger down the street, pack a lunch and head out to one of the area's many greenways for a relaxing break from the office or that tiresome convention. Or plan ahead and take a small group of your business comrades on a nearby hike in one of the area's many state parks. A well planned half-day get-away is the perfect complement to a business stay in the Triangle area.

60 Hikes Within 60 Miles:

RALEIGH

Alleghany Ramble

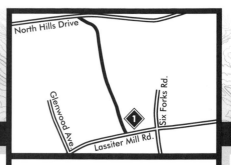

IN BRIEF

This hike takes in three of Raleigh's best greenway paths in addition to a jaunt through a local neighborhood. Along the way, you can enjoy views of Crabtree Creek and walk underneath the Beltline and listen to the cars and trucks rumble overhead.

DIRECTIONS

In Raleigh, park in the gravel lot at Aldert Root School, located on Lassiter Mill Road.

DESCRIPTION

On 5 September 1996, Hurricane Fran breached North Carolina from its southern Atlantic coast and turned Raleigh on its ear. In Raleigh and surrounding Wake County, Fran damaged and destroyed property valued at $900 million. As you walk this greenway path, note that you are walking along one of the many tributary creeks of Crabtree Creek, which experienced significant flooding and caused extensive damage when Fran roared through.

Begin the hike by taking an unnamed greenway path located just to the left of the gravel parking lot. This trail will lead you to a sidewalk at the intersection of Brunswick and Northampton Streets, about 0.1 mile from the trailhead.

Turn right onto Northampton and walk past the school. This sidewalk portion of the hike is 0.3 mile in length. Just

KEY AT-A-GLANCE INFORMATION

Length:
3.6 miles

Configuration:
Balloon

Difficulty:
Easy

Scenery:
Crabtree Creek

Exposure:
Part shade/part sun

Solitude:
None; this trail is exceptionally popular with cyclists and skaters.

Trail surface:
Paved

Hiking time:
1.3 hours

Access:
No fees or permits

Maps:
Capital Area Greenway Trail System Map or Raleigh Bike Map

Facilities:
None

9

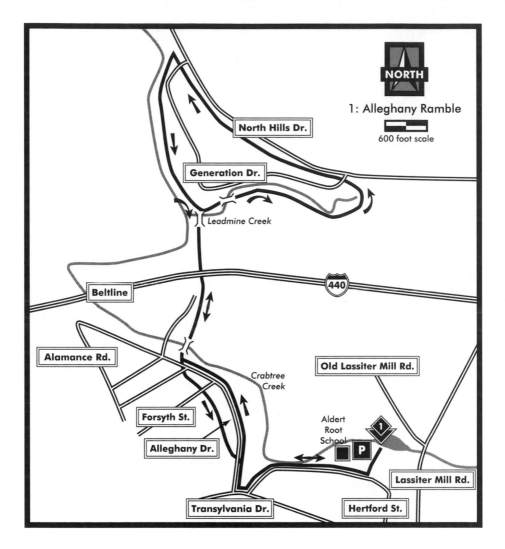

NORTH

1: Alleghany Ramble

600 foot scale

North Hills Dr.

Generation Dr.

Leadmine Creek

440

Beltline

Alamance Rd.

Old Lassiter Mill Rd.

Crabtree
Creek

Forsyth St.

Aldert
Root
School

1

P

Alleghany Dr.

Lassiter Mill Rd.

Transylvania Dr.

Hertford St.

beyond the school, the road swings to the left and changes names again, this time from Northampton to Hertford. Just follow the sidewalk. Be sure not to miss the view of Lassiter Mill that appears between the houses on your right. Lassiter Mill was built in the 1800s by local Raleigh entrepreneur Isaac Hunter and was used to grind corn into meal. The building later became Bloomsbury Park, a carnival-style park that incorporated the millstone wheel as the base of a merry-go-round. After an accident, the park was closed and the mill sold to Cornelius Lassiter.

Continue along the sidewalk, and after passing several homes, look for a Raleigh Greenway sign on the right. Take the steps down to the sandy path that parallel Crabtree Creek. You are now on the Alleghany Greenway Trail, which is 0.9 mile long.

Follow the Alleghany Greenway past the Yadkin Drive bridge. Just before the trail ends, you'll see a spur trail to your right. Take this spur trail to the Beltline

10

View these lichen-covered rocks along the Alleghany Greenway.

bridge and beyond. When you cross underneath the Beltline, you cross onto the North Hills Greenway, which is shaped like a U. Turn right and follow Lead Mine Creek. In half a mile you'll come to North Hills Drive. Turn left again and walk down North Hills Drive until you see the west entrance to the North Hills Greenway. Turn left. Soon you'll rejoin the spur that links the Alleghany Greenway to North Hills. Turn right and retrace your steps to Aldert Root School.

American Beech Trail

IN BRIEF

This gravel trail in Raven Rock State Park is perfect for young children. A cleverly designed interpretive station, located about halfway through the hike, helps the young ones distinguish between the various trees. Although the trail has sustained heavy storm damage in recent years, it still has enough trees to make the jaunt worthwhile.

DIRECTIONS

From Raleigh: Travel south on US 401 to Lillington. At the intersection of US 421 and US 401 in downtown Lillington, turn right onto US 421. Follow the signs to Raven Rock State Park. Trails begin from the left, center, and right of the parking lot. The American Beech Trail begins on the right side of the parking lot, just off the Raven Rock Loop Trail.

DESCRIPTION

There is much to do at Raven Rock State Park, including fishing, camping, and horseback riding (though you have to supply the horses). There is, of course, good hiking, and most of it quite easy. Over 12 miles of trails wander through the 3,549-acre park, which straddles the hard, resistant rocks of the foothills and the softer rocks of the coastal plain. The American Beech Trail is the shortest in the park and the most family friendly.

KEY AT-A-GLANCE INFORMATION

Length:
1 mile

Configuration:
Loop

Difficulty:
Easy

Scenery:
Woods, hurricane damage

Exposure:
Shady

Solitude:
Busy on weekends

Trail surface:
Loose gravel

Hiking time:
12 minutes

Access:
No fees or permits

Maps:
Raven Rock State Park map

Facilities:
Rest rooms, picnic tables, water, snack machines

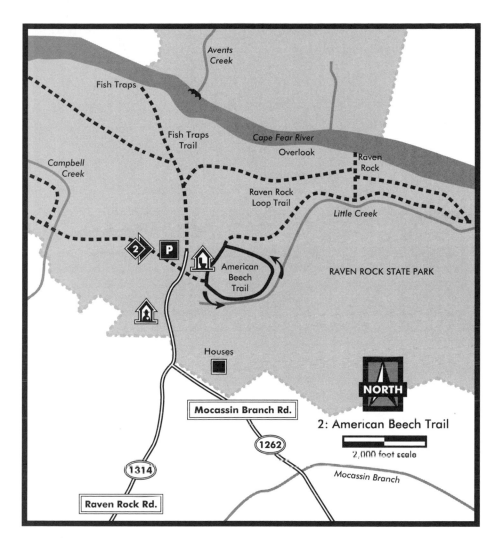

Avents Creek

Fish Traps

Fish Traps Trail

Cape Fear River

Overlook

Raven Rock

Campbell Creek

Raven Rock Loop Trail

Little Creek

2

P

American Beech Trail

RAVEN ROCK STATE PARK

Houses

NORTH

2: American Beech Trail

2,000 foot scale

Mocassin Branch Rd.

1262

1314

Mocassin Branch

Raven Rock Rd.

The longest is Campbell Creek Loop; see page 54.

The namesake of this hike, the American Beech, is abundant along this stretch of trail. To identify the tree, look for leaves that are almost egg-shaped, have coarse teeth around the edges, and are from one to five inches long. You might also recognize the bark, which is gray and smooth, though sometimes marred with carved names and initials of people who should know better than to carve on the trees. If you are hiking the trail during winter months, the beech trees will be easy to identify; the tree does not entirely shed its leaves. Also, look for tiny cigar-shaped buds on the twigs.

Although widespread and hardy, the American beech is vulnerable to disease. Beech bark disease has recently caused widespread tree loss in the Great Smoky Mountains National Park, and beech stands throughout the state have been damaged by a canker fungus known as Nectrina, which enters the tree through a breach in the bark—all the more reason to keep those initial-carving pocket knives sheathed.

Identify trees along the American Beech Trail with this lazy Susan tree finder.

This easy hike contains an interpretive station, reminiscent of a lazy Susan, about halfway along the trail. Kids can point an arrow at nearby trees—holly, poplar, sweet gum, red maple—and dial up information about them. It's a great little hike to cultivate outdoors enthusiasm in children.

As you walk along the trail, look for muscadine vines, lots of ferns, mountain laurel, and maple, poplar, and beech trees. It's possible you may see deteriorated stumps below the current hurricane damage; they are remnants from the days when this area was logged.

Durham Bulls Athletic Park

3

147

Cornwallis Road

American Tobacco Trail

IN BRIEF

Built on the old Norfolk and Southern Railroad line that once serviced the tobacco warehouses of Durham, the American Tobacco Trail just may be the best urban greenway hike in the Triangle. Lace up your shoes, go get the bike or rollerblades, and experience this wonderful trail!

DIRECTIONS

The northern terminus of the trail is located close to the Durham Bulls Athletic Park, just off NC 147 in Durham, near the corner of Blackwell and Morehead Streets. Parking is available in a small gravel lot underneath the bridge, across from the old tobacco warehouses. Cross Morehead Avenue to begin walking on the trail.

DESCRIPTION

Named after one of the city's early trademark firms—the American Tobacco Company—the smell of leaf tobacco in downtown Durham no longer tickles the pedestrian's nose. During the colonial period, though, tobacco was the most valuable export commodity of Durham and of North Carolina. Although the manufacture of tobacco products in Durham began prior to the Civil War, the first warehouse for the sale of leaf tobacco opened in 1871.

This nearly level hike south, full of long, straight stretches, is perfect for

KEY AT-A-GLANCE INFORMATION

Length:
6.4 miles
Configuration:
Out-and-back
Difficulty:
Moderate
Scenery:
Urban setting, hardwoods, kudzu
Exposure:
Sunny
Solitude:
None
Trail surface:
Asphalt
Hiking time:
2 hours
Access:
No fees or permits
Maps:
Durham Parks and Recreation Greenway Map
Facilities:
None
Special comments:
Once completed (scheduled for 2001) the trail should traverse three counties for 30 miles: Durham, Chatham, and Wake. The Triangle Greenways Council sees this trail as the backbone of a network of greenways stretching 70–100 miles that will allow people to commute via bicycle.

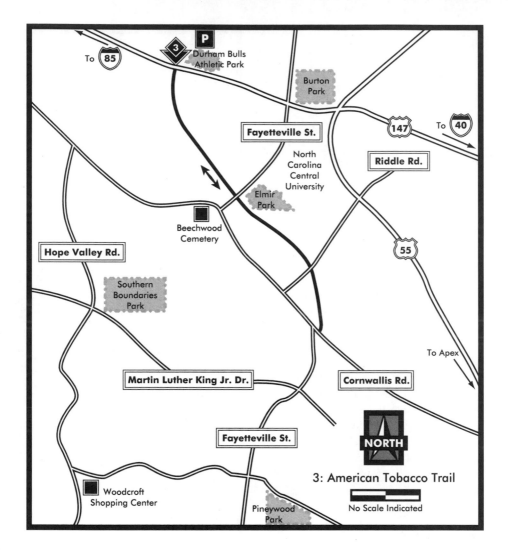

To 85

P

3

Durham Bulls
Athletic Park

Burton
Park

Fayetteville St.

147

To 40

North
Carolina
Central
University

Riddle Rd.

Elmir
Park

Beechwood
Cemetery

55

Hope Valley Rd.

Southern
Boundaries
Park

To Apex

Martin Luther King Jr. Dr.

Cornwallis Rd.

Fayetteville St.

NORTH

3: American Tobacco Trail

Woodcroft
Shopping Center

Pineywood
Park

No Scale Indicated

putting your feet in gear and letting your mind take a ride. The 6.4-mile trail follows the old railroad bed from downtown Durham to a point near Cornwallis Road. Along the way, you'll see typical urban sites—including a nice view of the Durham skyline on your return trip north—and pass over quite a few roads and creeks. You'll also cross Fayetteville Road; when you do, be sure to admire the bridgework. And, of course, you'll be hard-pressed not to see all of the kudzu that grows abundantly along the trail. Though you no longer smell the aroma of Bull Durham smoking tobacco wafting through town, if you go out hiking mid-morning you'll smell the ham biscuits and fried chicken from the Chicken Hut, a business about a block away from the Fayetteville Street crossing. It's sure to make your mouth water.

Bridge across the American Tobacco Trail.

Apex Reservoir Greenway

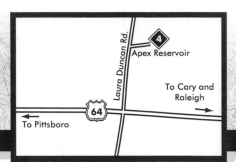

IN BRIEF

Very popular with moms pushing baby carriages, with runners, and with cyclists, this trail, which circles the Apex Reservoir, is one of the area's best lake hikes. It's neither too flat nor too hilly. If you're looking for a measured course featuring kilometer measurements, go here. The small town of Apex is located approximately ten miles southwest of Raleigh.

DIRECTIONS

From Raleigh: Follow US 64 west to Apex. Turn right where US 64 intersects Laura Duncan Road. The Apex Community Park is located 0.6 mile on the right. There is also a parking area for the trail off of Lake Pine Drive in Cary.

DESCRIPTION

Two miles long over mostly flat ground and lined with lots of pine trees, almost the entire way, this hike circles the Apex Reservoir. You'll see picnic tables and benches perfect for quiet contemplation or for just taking a break. You might also look for ducks and geese that sometimes visit the lake. Note, too, as you walk, that the hike feels more remote than it actually is. This is due in part to the thick stand of pines surrounding the lake. The south side of the trail is hillier than the north side, but neither is very difficult.

    Prior to the Civil War, Apex earned its name due to its location on the highest point of the Chatham Railroad, which

KEY AT-A-GLANCE INFORMATION

Length:
2 miles

Configuration:
Loop

Difficulty:
Easy

Scenery:
Excellent views of Apex Reservoir

Exposure:
Mostly shade; some sun when crossing the dam

Solitude:
Busy

Trail surface:
Asphalt

Hiking time:
45 minutes

Access:
No fees or permits

Maps:
None available

Facilities:
Rest rooms, water, picnic tables, ball fields

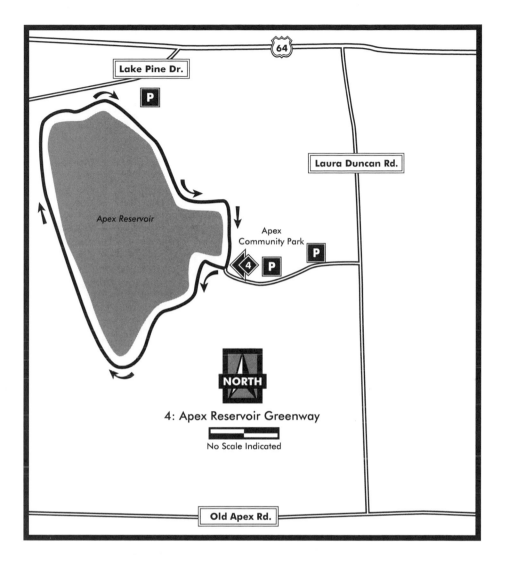

Lake Pine Dr.

64

Laura Duncan Rd.

Apex Reservoir

Apex
Community Park

P

4 P

P

NORTH

4: Apex Reservoir Greenway

No Scale Indicated

Old Apex Rd.

ran from Richmond, Virginia, to Jacksonville, Florida. If you visit downtown Apex, you'll notice a predominance of brick buildings. Two fires, one in 1905 and one in 1911, destroyed numerous commercial buildings constructed of wood. After the fires, storefronts along streets such as Salem were rebuilt as fireproof pressed-brick buildings.

Today, Apex's population is approximately 15,000 and growing, reflecting, perhaps, the town slogan: "Apex is the peak of good living."

Wake County itself is the fastest-growing county in North Carolina. Apex Reservoir, which forms the hub of this trail, is also known as Williams Creek Reservoir. Apex Reservoir is in an unprotected watershed and is not a current water supply source for Apex or Wake County. A town rich in water resources, rain which falls on Main Street in Apex either flows to the Neuse River or the Cape Fear River, depending on which side of the street it falls.

NEARBY ACTIVITIES

While you're in Apex, take advantage of the historic downtown walking tour given by the friendly Apex Historical Society. Call a few days in advance to set up a personal tour. The phone number is (919) 362-8980. If you're visiting in December, ask about the annual Christmas Tour of Homes, also hosted by the Historical Society.

If you're bringing children along for the hike, they may want to visit the Kidstowne Playground. After they've warmed up their legs on the Reservoir Trail, they should have a good time maneuvering through wooden mazes, swinging, or creating a castle in the sandboxes.

The playground is community funded and maintained for children of all ages. To visit, take Olive Chapel Road off NC 55. Go approximately 2.5 miles and turn left onto Kelly Road. The park will be on your left.

Art Museum Trail

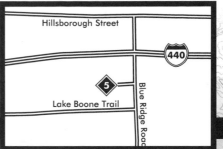

Hillsborough Street

440

5

Lake Boone Trail

Blue Ridge Road

IN BRIEF

Like a little bit of culture with your hike? If so, take time to pad along this trail: It's certainly one of a kind. Studded with sculpture by Thomas Sayre and other outdoor sculptures nearer the museum's entrance, this trail will give you lots of shapes to contemplate. It features unique views of Sayre's 24–foot-high sculpture, titled Gyre. Inside, the museum houses art collections of the State of North Carolina.

DIRECTIONS

The North Carolina Museum of Art (NCMA) is located on Blue Ridge Road between Wade Avenue and Lake Boone Trail, not far from the Interstate-40 ramp and the fairgrounds. The museum park trail is behind the museum, near the bottom of the last parking lot.

DESCRIPTION

A little-known trail, this hike edges the perimeter of the NCMA property and provides a view of Raleigh you've probably never seen. Though the Wade Avenue extension to I-40 is nearby, you probably won't hear too much of the traffic noise, thanks to a thick edging of trees.

Opened in June 2000, this bicycle and pedestrian path is described by the museum's director, Lawrence Wheeler, as "a museum without walls." Eventually this trail, and other trails, will connect to area greenways.

KEY AT-A-GLANCE INFORMATION

Length:
1.3 miles
Configuration:
Loop or out-and-back, your choice
Difficulty:
Easy
Elevation gain:
Minimal
Scenery:
Sculpture
Exposure:
Sunny
Solitude:
While not remote, this trail is not well known and tends to be empty.
Trail surface:
Paved
Hiking time: 25 minutes, more if you study the art
Access:
No fees or permits
Maps:
None printed; a sign at either end indicates the direction
Facilities:
Inside the art museum
Special comments:
Beware of hiking here when NCMA is hosting big events. Finding a parking spot can be difficult. The trail is open during daylight hours. Only walkers, cyclists, and pets on a leash may use the trail.

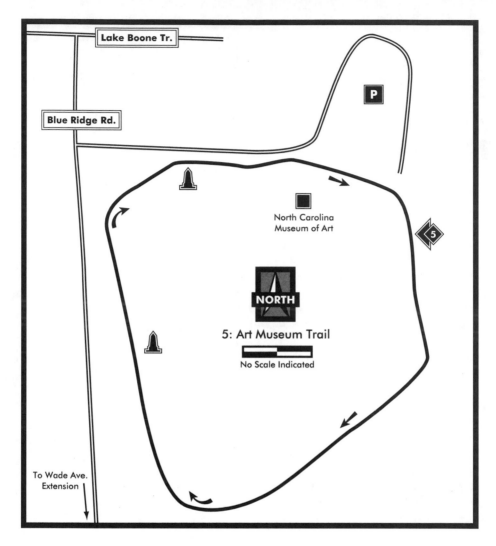

Lake Boone Tr.

Blue Ridge Rd.

P

North Carolina
Museum of Art

NORTH

5: Art Museum Trail

No Scale Indicated

5

To Wade Ave.
Extension

Near the end of the trail, you'll pass by the outdoor stage used by NCMA to host outdoor movies and various performances. Both the movies and the performances provide yet another reason to visit this museum. Over time, NCMA plans to enrich this trail by adding more sculptures.

NEARBY ACTIVITIES

If you develop an appetite after your walk, and happen to be wearing dressier walking clothes, then the Blue Ridge Restaurant, located on the bottom floor of the museum, is a handy destination. The artsy yet filling fare is best described as Provençal. After you partake of some bouillabaisse and a glass of Beaujolais, you might enjoy wandering the galleries, taking in the art. (If you like the outdoors, be sure to see the Bierstadt painting contained in the American galleries.)

Admission to the museum's permanent collection is free, although there is typically a charge for special exhibits. Call ahead for information at (919) 833-3548.

Sculpture along the Art Museum Trail.

Bald Mountain Trail

To Greensboro
6
Old State Rd. 86
Eubanks Rd.
Exit 266
1009
40
To Raleigh
To Chapel Hill

IN BRIEF

Like to look for the big trees? Then head over to Orange County to hike the Bald Mountain Trail. Along the way, you'll see one of the biggest poplar trees in the area. And don't let the term *mountain* fool you; there's relatively little elevation gain on this Duke Forest hike.

DIRECTIONS

Finding this parcel of Duke Forest is the tricky part of the hike. From Raleigh and Durham, drive west on Interstate-40. Exit onto Exit 266. Drive as if you're going into Chapel Hill. However, at the first stoplight, turn right onto Eubanks Road. Follow Eubanks Road until it dead-ends onto Old NC 86, which is also marked as NC 1009. Turn right and travel about a mile. The Bald Mountain trailhead will be on your left.

Parking is practically nonexistent at the gate, so be careful as you park on the side of the road.

DESCRIPTION

This easy hike is notable for the forest it passes through. First you'll ascend a gentle hill; later you'll ascend another ridge. As you walk up the first hill, look for a huge—and I mean huge—poplar tree to your right. It's about halfway in and is easily 15 feet in diameter. If you hike here in the spring, you can enjoy the lavender irises that bloom at its base, as well as the many witch hazel trees nearby.

KEY AT-A-GLANCE INFORMATION

Length:
2.2 miles

Configuration:
Out-and-back

Difficulty:
Easy

Scenery:
Forest chock full of larger-than-usual poplar, oak, and hickory trees

Exposure:
Mostly shady

Solitude:
Remote

Trail surface:
Gravel, grass

Hiking time:
45 minutes

Access:
No fees or permits

Maps:
Duke Forest

Facilities:
None

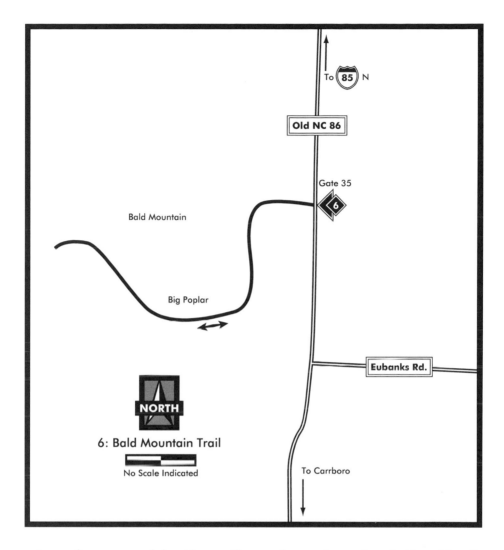

To (85) N

Old NC 86

Gate 35

6

Bald Mountain

Big Poplar

↔

NORTH

6: Bald Mountain Trail

No Scale Indicated

Eubanks Rd.

To Carrboro

Later, after you ascend the ridge, you'll continue walking down the other side until the trail dead-ends above a large open area. While the views aren't much to speak of—this is the Piedmont after all, not the western mountains—you'll get an excellent sense of how the Piedmont begins to roll. A forest heavily studied and managed since the 1930s by Duke University, a wealth of information about it and its flora and fauna is available to the public. Birds you may see while hiking include crows, robins, flycatchers, downy woodpeckers, wild turkeys, and screech owls. Also, whitetail deer are a common sight in the forest.

Duke Forest occupies 7,900 acres of land in many different and scattered parcels. A network of trails and forest service roads make the forest easily accessible. However, many of the forest's trails have been closed due to damage inflicted by Hurricane Fran in 1996.

NEARBY ACTIVITIES

While you're in the area, visit the Duke University Primate Center. Tours are available (by appointment) Monday–

Friday, 8:30 a.m. to 3 p.m., and Saturday, 8:30 a.m. to 1 p.m. The center's residents consist of prosimians, primarily big-eyed, nocturnal lemurs from Madagascar. To reach the Primate Center, travel east from I-40 on the US 15/501 bypass toward Interstate 85. Turn left onto NC 751. The Primate Center is located on the next left, which is Erwin Road. To arrange a tour, call (919) 489-3364. The center asks that you speak with a staffer and confirm a time and date at least two weeks in advance. Fees are $6 for adults and $3 for children ages 3 to 12. There are special rates for toddlers, seniors, and students.

Battle Branch/ Bolin Creek Ramble

Franklin Street

To Durham

15

Estes Drive

501

7

IN BRIEF

This hike, which combines two Chapel Hill greenways, truly has it all: rocks, creeks, cultivated rose gardens, and ham biscuits so close by you'll be tempted to stop hiking.

DIRECTIONS

Go to the Community Center in Chapel Hill, located just off Estes Drive near the Chapel Hill Mall. Park in the main lot. The Bolin Creek Greenway begins on the right as you drive in. The Battle Branch Greenway begins behind the left corner of the Community Center. Park at the Community Center and decide which out-and-back path you'll walk. Because both greenways are three miles long, round trip, it doesn't matter which one you pick first.

DESCRIPTION

This hike is reminiscent of Doctor Jekyll and Mr. Hyde: One greenway is paved and landscaped, while the other is root-bound, rock-strewn, and rather wild for an urban greenway. So, a pair of light hiking boots might be preferable over walking or tennis shoes.

The Bolin Creek Greenway is the Dr. Jekyll of the hike. It's paved and landscaped in sections, and passes by one of the area's prettiest rose gardens. The only problem with this portion of the hike is the smell of ham biscuits wafting down from the Sunrise Biscuit Shop, which is

KEY AT-A-GLANCE INFORMATION

Length:
6.1 miles
Configuration:
Two out-and-back trails
Difficulty:
Moderate
Scenery:
Creeks
Exposure:
Part sun/part shade
Solitude:
Busy most any time
Trail surface:
Rocks, gravel, boardwalks, asphalt
Hiking time:
3 hours
Access:
No fees or permits
Maps:
Available from Chapel Hill Parks and Recreation
Facilities:
Rest rooms, water, and a great rose garden at Community Center Park
Special comments:
Dogs are welcome, but must be kept on a leash. The trail opens at 6 a.m. and closes 30 minutes after sunset.

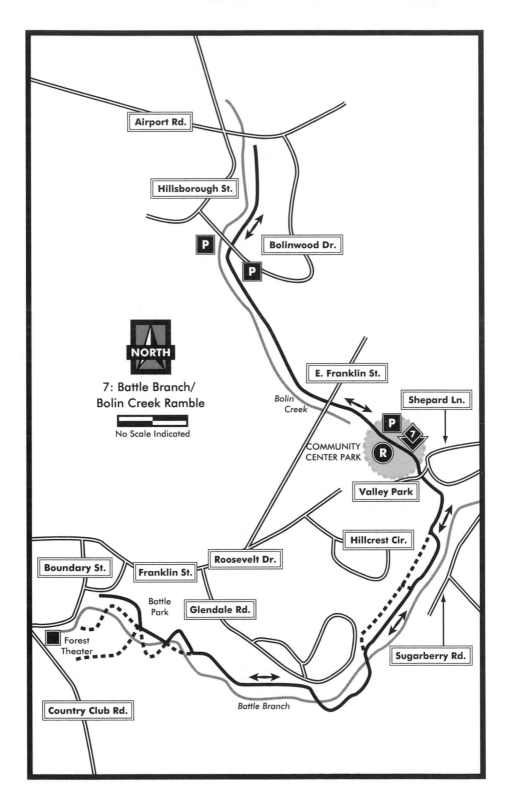

Airport Rd.

Hillsborough St.

Bolinwood Dr.

P

P

NORTH

**7: Battle Branch/
Bolin Creek Ramble**

No Scale Indicated

E. Franklin St.

*Bolin
Creek*

Shepard Ln.

P

7

COMMUNITY
CENTER PARK

R

Valley Park

Hillcrest Cir.

Boundary St.

Franklin St.

Roosevelt Dr.

Battle
Park

Glendale Rd.

Forest
Theater

Sugarberry Rd.

Country Club Rd.

Battle Branch

to your left just beyond the Franklin Street bridge. Not to worry, though: If you'll look to the left, among the rocks and kudzu, you'll see a path leading up to street level.

Follow the greenway to Airport Road, on the north side of town, then retrace your steps back to the Community Center Parking lot to finish this trail and begin the other.

Battle Branch is the Mr. Hyde: It's a wee bit difficult to follow. After you depart the center, you'll walk through a patch of woods, down a sidewalk, and then turn back into the woods. Here you'll see the Battle Branch Greenway has an upper and a lower trail. These two trails rejoin where the path intersects Glendale Road. The single path turns left, back into the woods.

The second portion of Battle Branch Greenway is the hard part. The trail is very rocky, and at times you'll need to either rock-hop across the creek or look for the upper path.

Soon you'll pass the remnants of a stone fireplace as well as some sort of sewer cone. Here, according to the map, the trail splits into three forks. Only the middle and right forks are obvious.

My advice is to take the right fork. The path is more evident and wider than the middle fork—which is a plus, given all the poison ivy along the trail. When you reach the intersection of Boundary Road and Park Place, you can walk to your left to see the Forest Theater.

Retrace your path back to the Community Center.

Beaver Dam/ Hymettus Woods Ramble

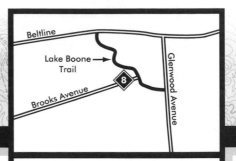

IN BRIEF

An excellent afternoon walk, this hike follows Beaver Dam Creek through some of the older neighborhoods of Raleigh. Though an urban walk located partly on sidewalks, it rambles among the hardwood trees of Beaver Dam Park on its way to Hymettus Woods, a little-used, often-overlooked city park that comes complete with a picnic table.

DIRECTIONS

Drive into Raleigh on Glenwood Avenue (US 70). Turn right onto Lake Boone Trail. Look for Brooks Avenue, which dead-ends on Lake Boone Trail. Park your car on Brooks Avenue. The trail starts on the corner of Lake Boone and Brooks Avenue.

DESCRIPTION

Begin on the sidewalk along Brooks Avenue. Soon you'll cross Beaver Dam Creek and walk along a footpath that's part of the park. When Brooks splits away from Banbury Road, stay in the park, walking along Banbury Road. Within Beaver Dam Park several bridges link the trail with picnic areas on either side of the creek. When you see a jungle gym and some picnic tables, leave the road and begin walking along a path that's just to the left of the creek. Follow this path until you get to Leonard Street.

At Leonard Street, continue walking left to where the path ends on Grant

KEY AT-A-GLANCE INFORMATION

Length:
2.8 miles

Configuration:
Out-and-back

Difficulty:
Easy

Scenery:
Beaver Dam Creek, Hymettus Woods Park, postwar neighbor-hoods

Exposure:
Sunny on the sidewalks, shady in the woods

Solitude:
Busy just about anytime

Trail surface:
Concrete, asphalt, dirt, gravel road

Hiking time:
1.3 hours

Access:
No fees or permits

Maps:
Capital Area Greenway Trail System Map or Raleigh Bike Map

Facilities:
Picnic table hidden within Hymettus Woods Park, jungle gym in Banbury Woods

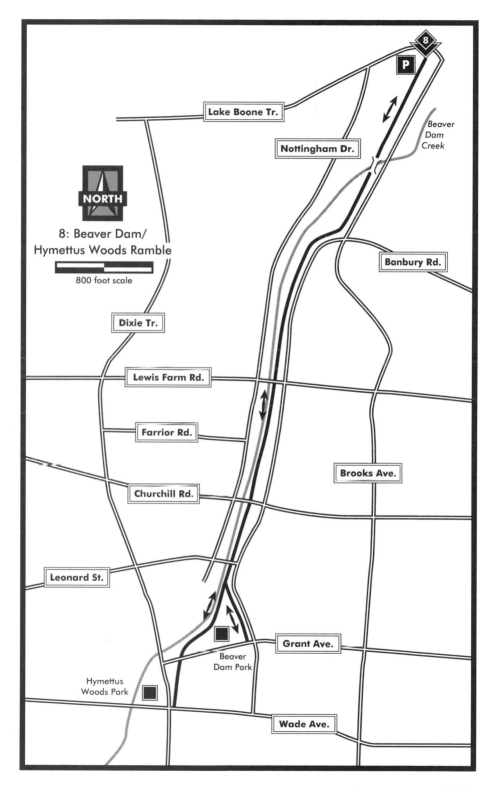

NORTH

8: Beaver Dam/
Hymettus Woods Ramble

800 foot scale

Lake Boone Tr.

Nottingham Dr.

Beaver
Dam
Creek

Banbury Rd.

Dixie Tr.

Lewis Farm Rd.

Farrior Rd.

Brooks Ave.

Churchill Rd.

Leonard St.

Grant Ave.

Beaver
Dam Park

Hymettus
Woods Park

Wade Ave.

Avenue. This out-and-back spur adds about 0.2 mile to your walk. When you come back to Leonard Street, look for a set of wooden steps on your left and take them. This part of the foot path leads into a wooded area and eventually pops out onto a gravel road.

Continue walking along the gravel road until it hits Dixie Trail. Here you can turn left and walk up to the light at the intersection of Wade Avenue and Dixie Trail. Cross onto Wade Avenue and walk about 0.1 mile to the entrance to Hymettus Woods Park. The name comes from Mt. Hymettus, a mountain rising to 3,367 feet in central Greece and known for its marble.

To return, retrace your steps back to Lake Boone Trail. The out-and-back trail length of 2.8 miles does not include hiking past Wade Avenue. For a treat after the hike, head to Hillsborough Street near North Carolina State University. You'll find numerous coffee shops and restaurants here. Or you might consider going up Wade Avenue to Wellspring Grocery, where people watching is a prime pastime.

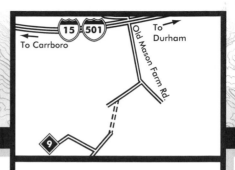

Big Oak Woods Trail

IN BRIEF

There's not another hike in the Triangle like this one. The 367-acre Mason Farm Biological Reserve, given to the University of North Carolina in 1894 by Mary Elizabeth Morgan Mason, has been undisturbed since the late 1700s.

DIRECTIONS

In Chapel Hill, turn onto Old Mason Farm Road off of the US 15/501 Bypass on the south side of town. Stop in at the Totten Center for your permit and then continue down Old Mason Farm Road.

When you enter the grounds of Finley Golf Course, keep a sharp eye for a turn to the right in front of the brick clubhouse. Don't let the signs indicating golf bag drop-offs confuse you. Make the right turn, and snake around the parking lot, making a left turn onto a gravel road at the southwest corner of the parking lot. When the road splits, take the right fork. Soon you'll come to a right turn, which goes across a concrete bridge. (Don't try fording the creek if you can't see the concrete or if your car has low ground clearance.) Ford the creek, and go up the hill, and look for the parking lot. The gravel road you see behind a gate is the trail.

When you leave, remember to blow your car horn before you start around the bushes to ford the creek. Sightlines are nonexistent, so you'll want to warn incoming vehicles what you're up to.

KEY AT-A-GLANCE INFORMATION

Length:
2 miles
Configuration:
Balloon
Difficulty:
Easy
Scenery:
Old farm fields reverting to forests, patches of old-growth forests
Exposure:
About 60% of the time you're out in the sun on this trail
Solitude:
Moderate
Trail surface:
Gravel roadbed
Hiking time:
1 hour
Access:
Permit required; available at the Totten Center in the North Carolina Botanical Garden. Call ahead at (919) 962-0522 for information.
Maps:
There's an old mailbox at the trailhead that contains laminated maps.
Facilities:
None
Special comments:
To reach the trailhead, you must ford a creek with whatever vehicle you drive; don't try this if you can't see the concrete.

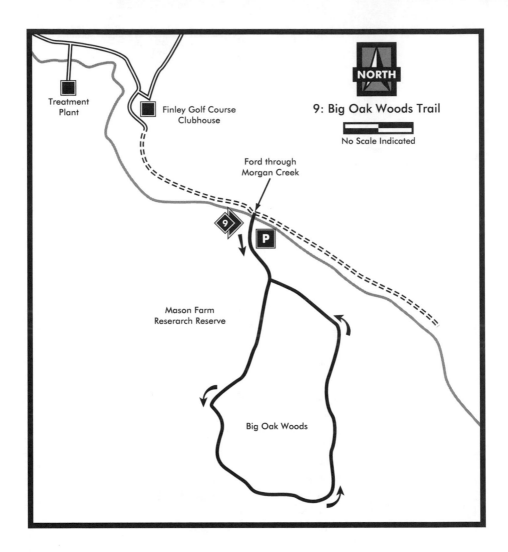

9: Big Oak Woods Trail

No Scale Indicated

Treatment Plant

Finley Golf Course Clubhouse

Ford through Morgan Creek

9

P

Mason Farm Reserarch Reserve

Big Oak Woods

Only one car can pass on the bridge at a time.

DESCRIPTION

As you walk the path, look for the blue stripes on the trees. If Jordan Lake were ever to flood, the stripes mark the boundary of a 100-year-level flood. (As the crow flies, you're less than 10 miles from Jordan Lake.)

One of the most interesting stations along the hike is at the top of the loop. Here, you'll see lots of big, dead trees. Morgan Creek, the creek you forded on

the way in, was "moved" by severe thunderstorms not long ago.

The beavers capitalized on the opportunity to stop the water flow and built dams and lodges. In doing so, they kept the area wet, and the trees, which were not accustomed to wet feet, died.

Some of the trees are thought to be 200 years old. Research in the area has yielded over 800 species of plants, 216 species of birds, 29 species of mammals, 28 species of fish, 28 species of snakes, 23 species of amphibians, and 67 species of butterflies. In recent years, this trail has had bobcat sightings as well as sightings of two albino deer.

As you return to the car, look in the woods to your left. Some of the pines and poplars in the wooded area there are huge. What really brings the naturalists to these woods, though, are the birds.

Black Creek Greenway/Lake Trail

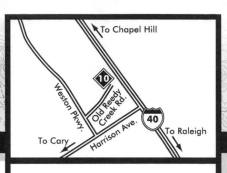

IN BRIEF

This 2.25-mile, paved Cary Greenway follows Black Creek from West Dynasty Drive (off Harrison Avenue) to Lake Crabtree. With lots of trees and a creek, this path is a serious contender for the most attractive urban greenway in the area.

DIRECTIONS

From Raleigh: Travel west on Interstate 40 and take Exit 287 onto Harrison Avenue. Turn left and travel toward Cary. Turn right where Weston Parkway intersects Harrison, just beyond the shopping center. Travel down Weston Parkway, turning right onto Old Reedy Creek Road. This road becomes a dirt road quickly. Continue on until the road turns back to pavement. Park your car along the road. Do not cross the bridge! (This is the locally famous "Bridge to Nowhere.") The trail begins just beyond the fence.

DESCRIPTION

From where you parked, cross the road, step inside the fence and begin walking to the left. (At this point the Black Creek Greenway and Lake Trail are following the same path. The trail you see to your right is a continuation of the Lake Trail.)

The Black Creek Greenway passes the southeastern side of Lake Crabtree before turning completely south. Just before the path crosses underneath West-

KEY AT-A-GLANCE INFORMATION

Length:
4.5 miles round-trip

Configuration:
Out-and-back

Difficulty:
Moderate

Scenery:
Interesting rock formations along Black Creek, great views of Lake Crabtree, possibility of seeing herons

Exposure:
Shady along Black Creek; 100% sunny at Lake Crabtree

Solitude:
Busy

Trail surface:
Paved

Hiking time:
1.3 hours

Access:
No fees or permits

Maps:
Cary Greenways Map

Facilities:
None

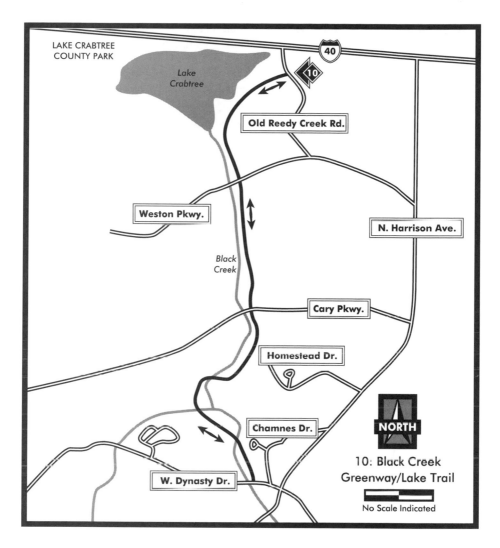

LAKE CRABTREE
COUNTY PARK

Lake
Crabtree

40

10

Old Reedy Creek Rd.

Weston Pkwy.

N. Harrison Ave.

Black
Creek

Cary Pkwy.

Homestead Dr.

NORTH

Chamnes Dr.

10: Black Creek
Greenway/Lake Trail

No Scale Indicated

W. Dynasty Dr.

on Parkway, Lake Trail splits to the right. The lake features shorebirds in August and September; at the marsh on the west end of the lake, killdeer, double-breasted cormorants, and the red-shouldered hawk are favorites of local birdwatchers.

Follow the path, paralleling Black Creek. If you want to look more closely at the creek, you can—but be careful. These woods are loaded with an exceptionally healthy crop of poison ivy! Along the way, you'll see spurs that lead out to various neighborhoods.

When you reach West Dynasty Drive, turn around and retrace your steps. Although the Cary Greenways map indicates that the trail continues to the right (up the hill) and then across the street, this section of the trail is not easy to find.

If you have enough life left in your legs when you reach the point where the Lake Trail rejoins the greenway, you can hike to the left along the Lake Trail. Doing so will add another 5.2 miles to your hike and will eventually bring you back to the starting point near the fence.

However, be aware that during periods of wet weather, this trail may be closed on the far side of the lake, meaning that you would have to retrace your steps to return to your car. (If the Lake Trail were closed and you hiked what amounted to an out-and-back around the lake, your total distance would exceed 12 miles.)

You can also park at the West Dynasty Drive end and walk the out-and-back from the south. The West Dynasty Drive entrance is near the intersection of Harrison Avenue and West Dynasty Drive.

NEARBY ACTIVITIES
While walking by Lake Crabtree, look for windsurfers and the latest craze in recreational lake adrenaline, the kiteboard. If you feel like getting out on the lake yourself, whether rowing or sailing, boat rentals range $5–10 an hour.

Bluff Loop/Stream Loop/ Discovery Loop Ramble

IN BRIEF

Located in Medoc Mountain State Park, this hike, found on the northwestern side of the park, traverses a high river bluff, recovering farmland, and a flood-plain forest. The bluffs you'll traverse are surprisingly high.

DIRECTIONS

Drive 25 miles north of Raleigh on US 401 to Louisburg. In Louisburg, turn right on NC 561 and travel another 30 miles to Hollister. In Hollister, follow the signs to Medoc Mountain State Park. Turn in at the first entrance you see. The trailhead begins behind the picnic shelter, over to the right.

DESCRIPTION

Medoc State Park contains five trails totaling nine miles. The short trails are easy hikes with occasional benches along the way.

Recent storms have changed the configuration of the Bluff Trail. Where it once was a loop, today it is a balloon hike. However, hike this trail first so that you can ascend and descend the bluffs while your legs are fresh.

It begins at the picnic area, taking you to Little Fishing Creek. If you have a valid North Carolina fishing permit, there are a few good fishing spots along the way.

The bluffs along Little Fishing Creek are impressive, and I recommend hiking

KEY AT-A-GLANCE INFORMATION

Length:
5 miles
Configuration:
The letter W
Difficulty:
Moderate
Scenery:
Creeks, high bluffs unusual to this area, reforested farmland
Exposure:
Mostly shady
Solitude:
You're apt to be alone here.
Trail surface:
Grass, roots, rocks, boardwalks
Hiking time:
2.5 hours
Access:
No fees or permits
Maps:
Available at the ranger station
Facilities:
Rest rooms, horseshoe pits, picnic tables, antique tobacco barn
Special comments:
This hike is composed of three separate trails: the 3-mile Bluff Trail, the 0.75-mile Stream Trail, and the 1.25-mile Discovery Trail. Recent storm damage has changed the configuration currently shown on maps. Call the park office at (252) 586-6588 for hours of operation.

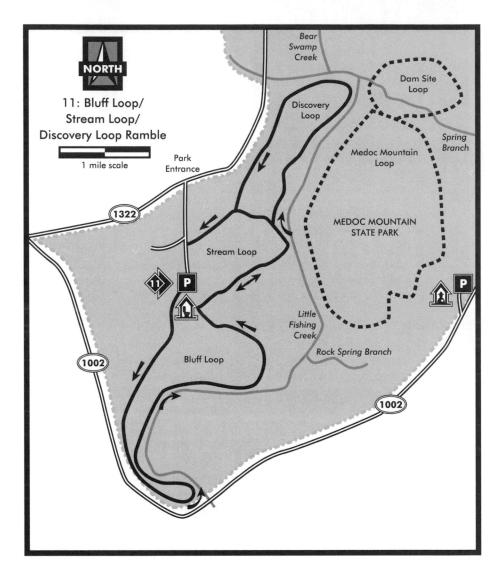

11: Bluff Loop/
Stream Loop/
Discovery Loop Ramble

1 mile scale

NORTH

Bear Swamp Creek

Discovery Loop

Dam Site Loop

Spring Branch

Medoc Mountain Loop

MEDOC MOUNTAIN STATE PARK

Park Entrance

1322

11

Stream Loop

Little Fishing Creek

Rock Spring Branch

Bluff Loop

1002

1002

this path during the late fall, winter, or early spring so that you can fully appreciate just how high the bluffs are.

Spring is the ideal time to enjoy the white and pink blooms of mountain laurel. Also, keep your eyes open for wildlife. On my second visit here, I spied a box turtle, which isn't that unusual. What was odd was seeing him hungrily eating a mushroom; he was so busy eating that he didn't bother closing up shop for me. Pretty bold behavior, I'd say, for a turtle.

After traversing the Bluff Trail, you can then add the 0.75 mile Stream Loop to your hike. The Stream Loop begins at the picnic area and follows the bank of Little Fishing Creek. The trail first descends to Little Fishing Creek and then curves back to the picnic area before intersecting the Discovery Loop.

When you reach the 1.25-mile Discovery Loop, turn left if you're ready to return to the picnic shelter. If not, turn right to walk through a floodplain forest.

Check out this Tobacco barn in Medoc Mountain State Park.

Look for shagbark hickory trees and water oaks through here, as well as running cedar. At the confluence of Little Fishing Creek and Bear Swamp Creek, the trail swings around to return to the picnic area. Guided hikes emphasizing natural history are available upon request.

NEARBY ACTIVITIES

Following your hike, have your lunch at the park's picnic area. There are 25 picnic tables and 10 grills here. A shelter with flush toilets may be reserved in advance.

If you like to fish, Little Fishing Creek has some fine bluegill fishing holes. Just bring a cane pole and a few worms.

Hollister, the nearest town, is home to the tribal council of the Halawi-Saponi Indians. The Halawi-Saponi tribe holds one of the largest pow wows in the state each year during April.

Bobbitt's Hole/ Cole Mill Trail

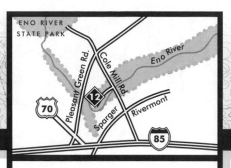

IN BRIEF
Located in Eno River State Park, this trail evokes lots of nostalgia. If the remains of a gristmill built in 1814 don't impress you, then perhaps the elbow bend in the river that looks like it made a perfect swimming hole in days gone by will.

DIRECTIONS
From Durham, travel west on Interstate 85. Exit onto Cole Mill Road. Just past the Eno River Bridge, turn left. Follow the road into the Cole Mill section. Park in the first parking area and walk first on the Cole Mill Trail. The trail for Bobbitt's Hole soon peels to the right about half a mile from the parking area. After hiking along Bobbitt's Hole Trail, return on Cole Mill Trail.

DESCRIPTION
Eno River State Park is nestled in a narrow river valley carved by the Eno River. The river is popular with paddlers, sporting rapids from Class I to III. The Eno is home to the Roanoke bass, a fish found in only three other rivers. Wildlife you may spot along trails include white-tail deer, raccoons, and opossum.

The best way to hike this trail is by walking first on the portion of the Cole Mill Trail that leaves from the upper parking lot. When you come to the red-blazed Bobbitt's Hole Trail, stay left on the Cole Mill Trail. In a short distance, you'll come to the Eno River.

KEY AT-A-GLANCE INFORMATION

Length:
2.65 miles from the parking lot

Configuration:
Loop

Difficulty:
Moderate

Scenery:
Excellent

Exposure:
Part shade/part sun

Solitude:
Moderate

Trail surface:
Dirt

Hiking time:
1.6 hours

Access:
No fees or permits

Maps:
Eno River State Park, Cole Mill Section

Facilities:
Rest rooms, water, picnic tables

Special comments:
All trails within the park are for pedestrians only. No bikes or horses allowed.

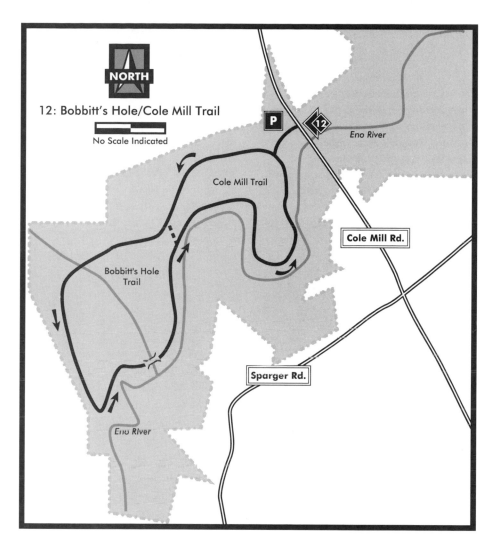

12: Bobbitt's Hole/Cole Mill Trail

No Scale Indicated

NORTH

Cole Mill Trail

Eno River

Cole Mill Rd.

Bobbitt's Hole Trail

Sparger Rd.

Eno River

When you reach the Eno River, turn right and walk upstream. The river will be on your left. Be sure to take in the high river bluffs covered with mountain laurel and Catawba rhododendron. Note also the tall, white sycamores that lean gracefully over the river. You'll find it hard to believe that this jewel of a trail exists in an urban area.

Soon you'll come to a spur that leads to Bobbitt's Hole. While swimming is no longer allowed, admiring this beautiful spot is still in order. Seldom will you see

such a picturesque, 90-degree bend in a river.

As you continue walking, note the tremendous number of downed trees, but don't let it concern you. Because more sun strikes the forest floor, this portion of the trail is the quintessential Christmas hike. Sun-loving, volunteer hollies, many with red berries, grow thickly in this area. No hike in the Triangle area matches this one for the sheer number of evergreen hollies. You're also likely to see hawks and owls, hunting for their dinner.

43

After leaving Bobbitt's Hole, rejoin the lower portion of Cole Mill Trail for a hike at the river's edge along the Eno. This portion of the trail is the hardest: The river and the high bluffs on the other side are a feast for the eyes, but the trail has tricky footing due to roots and moisture. You'll see places where other hikers have created walk-arounds to dodge the sometimes-too-slippery path. Hang on to the kids through here.

Look for the huge rock out-croppings on the far side of the river. This is where John Cole operated his gristmill in the late 1800s. As you round the bend and begin walking back toward the parking lot, be sure to smell the river water. Because of the rapids churning the water, you'll be able to smell it quite easily.

Guided tours and interpretive programs are available upon request. Call ahead for scheduling, (919) 383-1686.

NEARBY ACTIVITIES

At the access area of Cole Mill, there is a picnic shelter with grill. There are also several outdoor picnic tables and grills available for picnickers.

Bond Fitness Trail

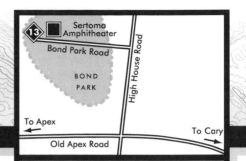

Sertoma
Amphitheater
Bond Park Road

High House Road

BOND
PARK

To Apex
←

Old Apex Road

To Cary

IN BRIEF

Located in the Fred G. Bond Metro park, a 310-acre facility, this hike features 5 miles of foot paths, a 42-acre lake, athletic fields, a playground, and picnic shelters. The Bond Fitness Trail is not only a good walk; it also offers 20 fitness stations along the way.

DIRECTIONS

From downtown Cary, drive west on Chatham Street. Just out of downtown, Chatham Street bears to the left. Stay straight on Old Apex Road. At the intersection with High House Road, turn right. Bond Park is 1.3 miles on the left.

The Bond Park Fitness Trail is accessible from several spots in the park. However, if you like to start at the beginning, drive until you see the arrows pointing to the amphitheater. Turn right and park. Walk down the hill and cross the parking lot associated with Field No. 3 to find the beginning of the Fitness Trail.

DESCRIPTION

This trail and park are named after former Cary Mayor Fred G. Bond. Bond served the tobacco industry for 43 years, including 23 years as Chief Executive Officer of the Flue-Cured Cooperative Stabilization Corporation. The Georgia native served on the Cary Town Council for 18 years, 12 as mayor.

This pleasant, wood-chip trail forms a loop on the northwest side of Cary's

KEY AT-A-GLANCE INFORMATION

Length:
1.5 miles
Configuration:
Loop
Difficulty:
Easy, unless you include those workout stations
Scenery:
Lots of maples trailside make for a colorful fall hike.
Exposure:
Part sun/part shade
Solitude:
Often busy
Trail surface:
Wood chips; can be soppy after wet weather
Hiking time:
30 minutes
Access:
No fees or permits
Maps:
Available on a board near the amphitheater
Facilities:
Rest rooms, water, kid-friendly playgrounds, ballfields
Special comments:
Due to the shortness of trails mountain bikers tend to frequent other trail areas. Heavy jogger traffic in the morning and evening make midday the best time to take a hike.

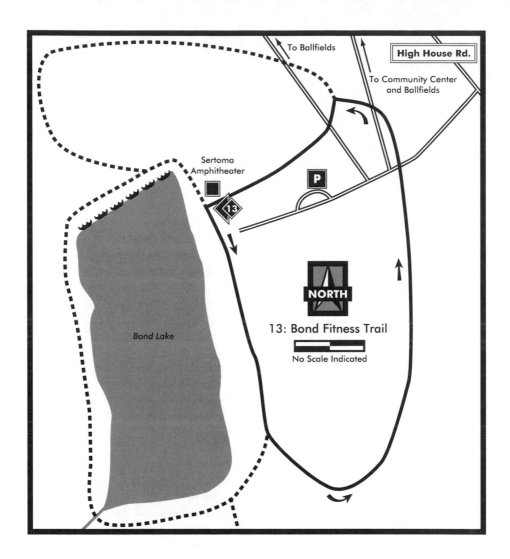

To Ballfields

High House Rd.

To Community Center and Ballfields

Sertoma Amphitheater

P

13

NORTH

13: Bond Fitness Trail

No Scale Indicated

Bond Lake

Bond Park. The only real challenge—other than the workout stations—is not letting the other overlapping trails confuse you.

Once you're on the trail, because it is a loop, follow it in either direction. Soon enough you'll see signs and stations for the 20 workout exercises. If you're feeling frisky, add them in. Since I'm the kid who's always in the creek, I make sure to walk the balance beam. (Not that the extra practice has kept me out of all of the creeks.)

Along the way, you'll have a few long-range views of Bond Lake and several of the baseball fields. The park is open daily from 9 a.m. to sunset.

NEARBY ACTIVITIES

If you've wanted to hike outdoors without the aid of trails, then a short course in orienteering is the place to start. Monthly orienteering courses are offered at the park. There is a small fee of $3 for Cary residents and $5 for non-residents. The fee includes a color map, punch card, and use of a compass. Call the Bond Park Community Center for more information at (919) 469-4100.

Pedal boats, fishing boats, canoes, and sailboats are available for rent by the hour. One person 16 years of age or older must be in the boat at all times. Call ahead for rental hours and fees at (919) 469-4100.

For a bite to eat following your hike, visit nearby Bruegger's Bagel Bakery. Located at 4212 NW Cary Parkway, Bruegger's offers more than a dozen bagel flavors and their own brand of java.

Bond Lake Loop

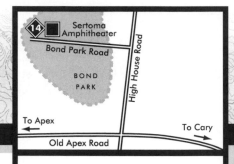

IN BRIEF

This hike is a combination of the 2.5-mile loop around Bond Lake, the 1.5-mile Oxford Hunt Greenway, and another 2-mile loop hike in Bond Park in Cary.

DIRECTIONS

From downtown Cary, drive west on Chatham Street. Just out of downtown, Chatham Street bears to the left. Stay straight, however, on Old Apex Road. At the intersection with High House Road, turn right. Bond Park is 1.3 miles on the left. Park in the lot near the Sertoma Amphitheater.

DESCRIPTION

From the parking lot, walk down the wood-chip path by the amphitheater to the gravel road. Here you'll see a post with red, yellow, blue, and green triangles. (Several trails come together here.)

Hike left, following the blue triangle. You'll soon pass a boat ramp and the stand where pedal boats can be rented. Follow the trail up the hill to the left, where it again becomes a wide gravel path. You'll also see a sign marking the end of the Oxford Hunt Greenway, a private greenway that is open to public use.

Walk right, following the blue triangles. Within about 30 yards, the red and yellow trails split away to the left. You, however, will continue walking to the right. Your next landmark is where the

KEY AT-A-GLANCE INFORMATION

Length:
7.5 miles if you walk it all. The Bond Lake loop is 2.5 miles; the Oxford Hunt Greenway adds another 3 miles if walked as an out-and-back; the Bond Park Red Trail adds another 2 miles.

Configuration:
Figure 8

Difficulty:
Moderate due to distance; the terrain is easy.

Scenery:
Lake views, large patches of Virginia spiderwort in late April and early May; possibly lots of turtles

Exposure:
Mostly deep shade

Solitude:
Busy

Trail surface:
Wood chips, gravel paths, roots, pine needles

Hiking time:
1 hour

Access:
No fees or permits

Maps:
Trail sign at the Sertoma Amphitheater

Facilities:
Rest rooms, water, kid-friendly playgrounds, ballfields

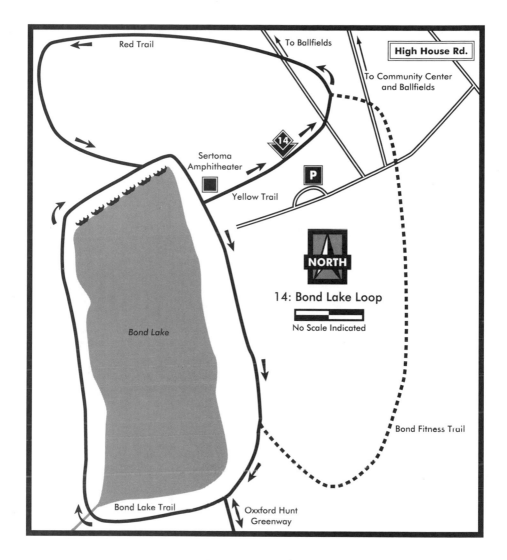

Red Trail

To Ballfields

High House Rd.

To Community Center
and Ballfields

Sertoma
Amphitheater

14

P

Yellow Trail

NORTH

14: Bond Lake Loop

No Scale Indicated

Bond Lake

Bond Fitness Trail

Bond Lake Trail

Oxxford Hunt
Greenway

Oxford Hunt Greenway splits away from the Bond Lake Trail. You can hike this path as an out-and-back spur, adding three miles to your distance. Sights you'll see along the way include an inside look at what some of Cary's residents are up to, including well-kept apartment complexes, swim clubs, "middle-class mansions," and some pleasant landscaping.

When you rejoin the Bond Lake Loop, hike left, behind several homes. You may hear a few yard dogs barking and maybe see a stray cat or two, but there's nothing to worry about. On the western side of the lake, look for patches of Virginia spiderwort blooming mid-spring.

Soon you'll cross the dam and find yourself heading back to the gravel road near the boathouse where the four trails come together. If your feet aren't barking too loudly, keep following the blue trail. This time, however, when the red and yellow trails split to the left, you're going to jump track onto the red and yellow trail.

For the next mile, you'll walk along

this combination path. When you reach the back corner of the community center, the yellow trail will turn left. However, continue along the red trail.

Eventually the red trail comes back around to connect with the Bond Lake Trail just below the dam. Once again you'll walk up the gravel road below the boathouse. But this time turn left up the wood-chip path to return to your car.

NEARBY ATTRACTIONS

If your appetite calls for more than a bagel and coffee, head to High House Road, which borders Bond Park.

Restaurants include China Gate, 986 High House Road, (919) 319-1818); Mancinos Pizza & Grinders, 1937 High House Road, (919) 481-6775); and Jersey Mike's Giant Submarines, 957 High House Road, (919) 461-0660.

Buckquarter Creek Trail

IN BRIEF

In addition to passing over ground with an interesting, pre–Revolutionary War history, this hike also provides stunning deck views of the Eno. Kids will like this hike: Lots of gnawed tree stumps left by area beavers stud the area near the top of the loop.

DIRECTIONS

From Durham, take Interstate 85 west Exit onto US 70 West. Almost immediately, turn right onto Pleasant Green Road. Turn left at the intersection with Cole Mill Road and follow Cole Mill until it ends in the Few's Ford section of Eno River State Park. Turn right into the first (and also unmarked) parking lot beyond the ranger station. Look for a sign that says River Access Trails, below and in front of the Piper-Cox Cabin. The orange-blazed Buckquarter Creek Trail peels to the right of Few's Ford.

DESCRIPTION

This trail is one of three located in the Few's Ford area of the Eno River State Park. At Buckquarter Creek, you can walk across the creek to join Holden's Mill Trail (4.1 miles). However, continue on the Buckquarter Creek Trail to loop back to your starting point.

As you leave the parking lot and walk down to the trailhead, be sure to note the shallow ford in the river. You are

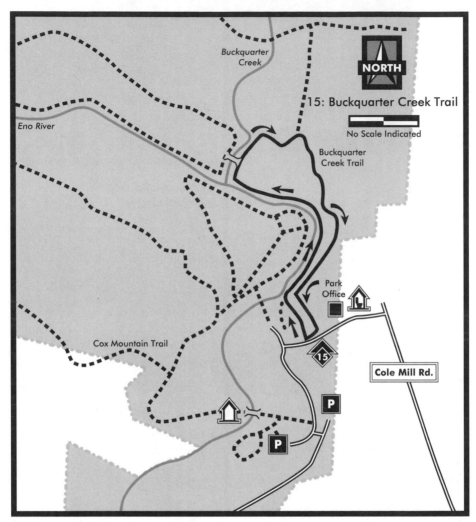

Buckquarter
Creek

15: Buckquarter Creek Trail

No Scale Indicated

Buckquarter
Creek Trail

Eno River

Park
Office

Cox Mountain Trail

15

Cole Mill Rd.

P

P

walking on land that witnessed some of the area's earliest colonial history.

William Few, a prosperous Quaker from Pennsylvania, came to this area with his wife and his brother James in 1758. He bought 640 acres of land along the Eno River. After clearing the land and starting crops, he and James erected a gristmill, the remains of which you can see by fording the river and walking up the river bank to the left.

(The remnants can also be seen from Fanny's Ford Trail if you don't want to get your feet wet.)

Both men were politically active, James particularly so. James eventually became known as one of the Regulators, a group espousing colonial government tax reform. "Regulated" taxes, they thought, would at least be fair taxes. In this way, the Regulators were forerunners of the Revolutionary War patriots.

The issue of taxation came to a head in the spring of 1771, with Governor Tryon sending troops to overwhelm the Regulators. After a skirmish at Alamance Creek some miles to the west, James Few was caught and hanged. Later, on

Eno River rapids along the Buckquarter Creek Trail.

his way home, Tryon turned William Few's cattle and horses loose into the family's planted fields as punishment for James's involvement. Shortly afterward, the Few family pulled up stakes and moved to Georgia.

After leaving the trailhead, follow the trail along the riverside and up, around, and over seriously large boulders. If you hike after heavy rains, footing is likely to be tricky. Along the way, you'll see lots of rocky ledges that make for good photo opportunities. After the initial boulder scramble, the trail gently rolls through an area where beavers are active. You won't have to look hard to find gnawed stumps!

At the top of the loop, the trail circles back through abandoned farmland. You'll know you're in the area when you see a grove of gnarled cedars, some quite large. Finally, as you near the end, you'll walk along the high river bluffs in thickets of mountain laurel while the Eno River, below and to the right, splashes its way eastward.

Campbell Creek Loop/Lanier Falls

IN BRIEF

This is one of my favorite hikes! This 6-mile moderate hike in Raven Rock State Park passes through holly forests, follows old roadbeds once used by ferry traffic, and winds along Campbell Creek. A 0.4-mile spur on the Campbell Creek Loop leads to Lanier Falls, a series of ledge rapids spanning the Cape Fear River.

DIRECTIONS

From Raleigh: Travel south on US 401 to Lillington. At the intersection of US 421 and US 401 in downtown Lillington, turn right onto US 421. Follow the signs to Raven Rock State Park. Campbell Creek Loop begins to the right of the parking area.

DESCRIPTION

Raven Rock State Park lies in the Cape Fear River Basin, a zone where the foothills meet the coastal plain. The shift in geology is largely responsible for the wide variety of plant and animal life in the area. The primary objective of most hikers is to combine this trail with the Lanier Falls Trail to view the falls overlook. The trail begins first by passing through a pine thicket, which shows signs of having been burned. The trail then descends to Campbell Creek, where you'll cross a large wooden footbridge. Beyond the bridge, the loop begins.

If you hike to the right, you'll follow Campbell Creek as it meanders to the

KEY AT-A-GLANCE INFORMATION

Length:
6 miles, including the out-and-back spur to Lanier Falls

Configuration:
Loop and spur

Difficulty:
Moderate

Scenery:
Excellent river views, creeks

Exposure:
Part shade/part sun

Solitude:
Moderately busy on weekends

Trail surface:
Dirt, gravel

Hiking time:
2.75 hours

Access:
No fees or permits

Maps:
Raven Rock State Park

Facilities:
Rest rooms, water, picnic tables, snack machines

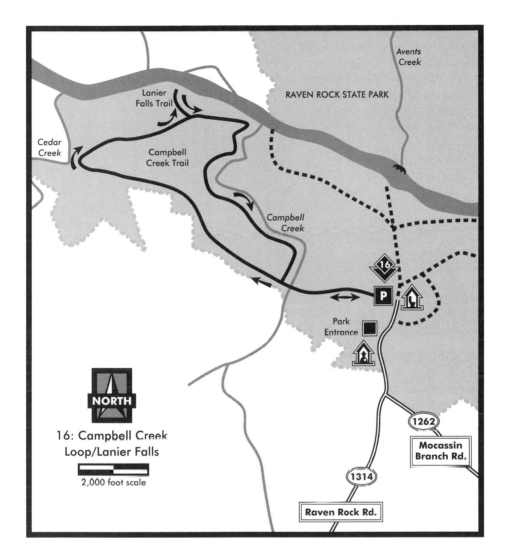

16: Campbell Creek Loop/Lanier Falls

2,000 foot scale

Cape Fear River. If you go left, you'll hike through moderately rolling ridges. Hiking left means hiking the most difficult part of the trail first, which isn't a bad idea, given the length.

After passing through holly trees and a mixed woods forest, you'll arrive at a sharp turn to the right in the trail. Hurricane damage has opened up the views somewhat and you can see the split in the trees indicating where the Cape Fear flows. The white blazes you see directly across the trail belong to the mostly abandoned Buckhorn Trail. Turn right and approach the Cape Fear River on an old roadbed.

The Cape Fear meanders through the North Carolina Piedmont for 200 miles. Two rivers, the Deep and the Haw, converge near Moncure to form the Cape Fear. After flowing through an estuarine environment, the Cape Fear empties into the Atlantic Ocean near Southport.

As you approach the river, river birch, sycamore, and beech trees shade the way. Listen for the calls of wood ducks, and keep your eyes open for small lizards and a wide variety of non-poisonous snakes, including the rat snake or the eastern hognose. Most of the snakes are harmless, but a few hikers may catch a rare glimpse of poisonous varieties such as the copperhead.

A family camping area appears on the left. There are five camping sites, each accommodating four persons. The sites contain tent pads and fire circles. If the woods are not your idea of a powder room, there is an outhouse here. Camping permits may be obtained at the park office. Just moments beyond the camping area, the spur to Lanier Falls comes into view. It's only about 300 yards, so be sure to take it. The falls, rated as Class I rapids, are quite scenic. Unless you have a telephoto lens on your camera, though, they'll prove hard to shoot. After passing the Lanier Falls spur, the loop swings around to follow Campbell Creek.

The park offers regularly scheduled educational programs and hikes. Contact the park office at (910) 893-4888 for more information on these programs.

Camp Durant Ramble

IN BRIEF

This hike on land that was once a Boy Scout camp sports the largest patch of wisteria in the area; if at all possible, hike here in mid-spring to see it. I promise you won't believe your eyes, so thick are the vines and flowers!

DIRECTIONS

From Raleigh, drive north on Falls of the Neuse Road. Turn right on Durant Road. The entrance to Durant Park is on a gravel road to the right, 1.4 miles from Falls of the Neuse Road.

DESCRIPTION

During the 1950s, Durant Park served as a Boy Scout camp. However, in 1979, the city of Raleigh bought the 237-acre property and turned it into a city park. Because of its use as a Boy Scout camp, you'll see several trails that weave in between the two main loops.

From the parking lot at the north entrance, hike down a short asphalt path to an information station. Here the path splits into two. Take the right path, which looks like an old roadbed and is marked with two blocks of wood, one indicating that bikes are allowed and the other painted with a pink lady's slipper (hikers only).

Soon the path splits again, with the bike trail going straight. You, however, will follow the pink lady's slipper. The trail descends a gentle hill, and for a

KEY AT-A-GLANCE INFORMATION

Length:
5.7 miles
Configuration:
Loop in a loop
Difficulty:
Easy
Scenery:
Lakes, beaver activity, interesting rocks, remains of former Boy Scout camp; homestead and farm remains
Exposure:
Mostly shady, except dam area
Solitude:
Busy on weekends; during the week can be busy in the spring when classes come out to study
Trail surface:
Some asphalt, mostly dirt
Hiking time:
1 hour
Access:
No fees or permits
Maps:
Xeroxed maps (at park office, left of the parking lot at north entrance)
Facilities:
Rest rooms, water, picnic tables
Special comments:
Outside the park is a 2.2-mile paved greenway path that can be added to form a single, 5.7-mile hike. If your legs are feeling springy and your dogs don't bark, go for it.

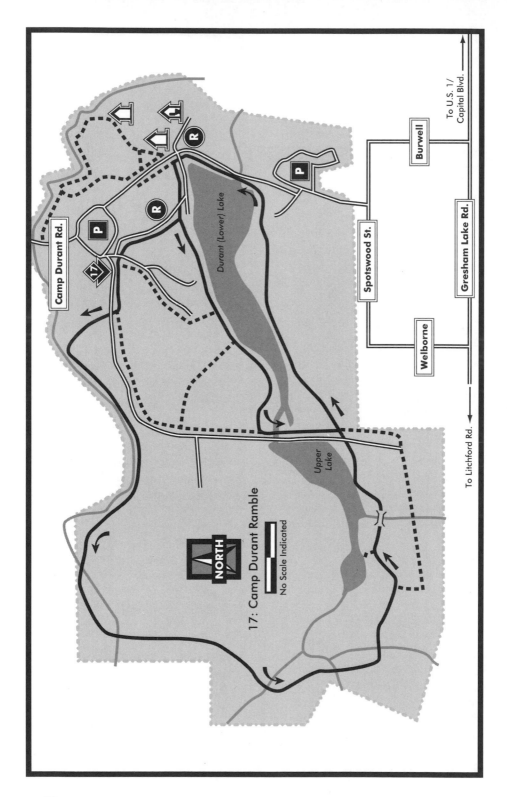

17: Camp Durant Ramble

NORTH

No Scale Indicated

Camp Durant Rd.

Durant (Lower) Lake

Upper Lake

Spotswood St.

Burwell

Welborne

Gresham Lake Rd.

To U.S. 1 /
Capital Blvd.

To Litchford Rd.

moment, you'll think you're about to join a Raleigh greenway path. When the trail reaches a small creek, however, turn left and limbo under a fallen tree to stay on the Border Trail.

As you walk alongside the creek, look for an unusual rock formation in the creek. What appear to be whales carved from stone are actually Whale Rocks. Through here, the trail passes behind several subdivisions, but there are enough trees and undergrowth that you won't feel as if you're trespassing in the homeowners' yards.

Soon the trail bends to the left and crosses a low, wet area before it begins a gentle ascent to an old homestead. In early spring, this trail cannot be beaten for flower interest. Evidently, the people who once lived here planted some wisteria; today, the vine is taking over the trees, and when the wisteria is in bloom, you'll feel like you're walking in a lavender fantasy. Note the size of the vines; some are as big as your arm. Just beyond the remains of a stone fireplace, the trail splits. Bear left to descend to the upper lake and to the beaver pond overlook.

Beyond the beaver pond overlook, follow Upper Lake to the right. Here you can see remains of diving platforms used by the scouts. When you see a path that's

marked with a bicycle block turning sharply to the right, turn to the right and pass by remnants of scout huts. Keep a sharp eye for concrete slabs where cabins used to stand. This trail descends and then ascends a gentle hill, before curving back to the left to another lake, Durant Lake.

Walk by Campbell Lodge (up the hill to your right), and cross the dam. Durant Lake, also called the Lower Lake, is to your left. Several picnic shelters and playing fields are to your right. At this point, you've completed the outside loop, for a total of 2.4 miles.

To include the inside loop, turn sharply to the left after crossing the dam to walk in front of the boathouse. This trail, marked with a cardinal, is the Lakeside Trail. Loop the lake, cross the dam between the Upper Lake and Durant Lake, and return to the first dam, below Campbell Lodge. When you pass the left turn to the lake, stay straight and walk up the hill to return to the parking lot at the north entrance. At this point, you will have hiked 3.5 miles.

After returning to the parking lot, walk down the gravel entrance road to the greenway path for the last 2.2 miles. The greenway path is 1.1 miles long. Hiking both sides as an out-and-back hike brings your total to 5.7 miles.

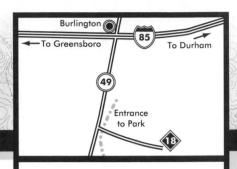

Cedarock Nature Trails Combo

IN BRIEF

If the kids are small or if they've never seen a preserved working farm, a trip here is certainly in order. Near the end of the hike, you'll walk by one of the area's best preserved grist mills.

DIRECTIONS

From Raleigh, drive west on Interstate 40. Before you get to Chapel Hill, exit onto NC 54 West and travel around Chapel Hill and Carrboro until you reach Interstate 85. Exit onto I-85 South, and drive until you see the exit for NC 49. Take NC 49 south about eight miles. Cedarock Park is on the left. From Durham, drive south on I-85 until you see the exit for NC 49.

Cedarock Park is just over 30 miles from Chapel Hill, 36 miles from Durham, and just over 60 miles from Raleigh.

To reach the hiking trails, turn in to the picnic area and park near shelter number three. There you'll see a board showing the trail system. Though the board makes it look, to quote my husband Randall, like you're "going to hike across Montana," the scale inside the park is very manageable.

DESCRIPTION

Ever heard of the Cane Mountains? Me neither. But in southern Alamance County, you can hike through what's left of them. Although they are quite worn

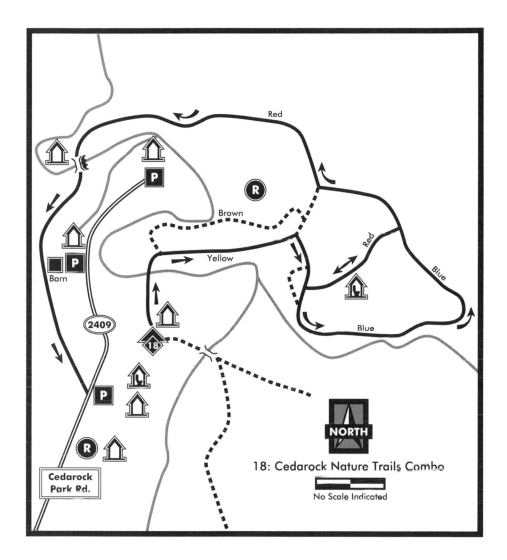

Red

Brown

Yellow

Red

Blue

Barn

2409

18

Blue

P

P

P

R

R

Cedarock
Park Rd.

NORTH

18: Cedarock Nature Trails Combo

No Scale Indicated

and pose no serious challenge to a hiker, you'll enjoy walking through the lush forest. The 400-plus-acre Cedarock Park was once a working farm. Several of the farm buildings, including the family home (built in 1835) corn crib, carriage barn, post office, and barns are still standing.

Hike first along the yellow trail. It leaves the picnic area, passes underneath some trees, and then crosses the bottom side of a small meadow before entering the woods again.

Upon entering the woods, you'll see the brown-marked Ecology Trail splitting off to the left. If the kids are small, a hike on the Ecology Trail will help them with their tree-identifying skills, since many of the trees are marked. The Ecology Trail rejoins the yellow trail farther up to make a loop.

On this hike, however, continue along the yellow-blazed trail until you come to the blue trail. Turn right onto the blue trail and begin following a little creek. This area is home to several spring wild-

Water flowing over dam in Cedarock Park.

flowers due to the moisture of the creek. When hiking there, I spied a wild Easter lily, which is also known as a Zephyr lily.

Soon you'll come to the red trail, splitting off to your left. Don't take it; continue hiking along the blue trail.

Soon, you'll cross the top of the trail and begin returning to the yellow trail. When you see the Red trail again, you can walk its 0.16-mile length as an out-and-back to add some mileage to your hike. After returning to the blue trail, you'll once again intersect the yellow trail.

When you near the end of the yellow trail, you'll hear what sounds like a mon-strous waterfall. As you near it, you'll see instead that what you hear is water splashing over a dam. Take time to look closely; you'll see all sorts of carved, stacked rocks. (If you do go down to view the dam, be careful along the rocks: They're a haven for poison ivy!)

After leaving the dam and gristmill, the trail passes by a gazebo and swings to the left through a field. It comes up behind a barn used as a maintenance shed, and crosses another grassy area and the park road. You'll then re-enter the woods, walk across the top of the meadow near the beginning of the hike, and see the lot where you're parked.

Company Mill Trail with Sycamore Loop

IN BRIEF
On this hike, you'll pass the remains of an old mill, scale the highest bluffs in the park, and walk beside two different creeks.

DIRECTIONS
From Raleigh, drive west on Interstate 40 and take Exit 287 onto Harrison Avenue. Turn right to go into Umstead State Park using the Reedy Creek entrance. The trail begins near the picnic tables on the northwest side of the park. Because these two trails traverse the width of the park, you can access the trail from the Crabtree Creek entrance, off US 70 in Raleigh.

DESCRIPTION
Here's the long-distance hike you're looking for. The first time I hiked this trail was a cool day in January. It was wonderful. Since that time, almost ten years ago, I go out each year to hike it again. If you've been cooped up too long inside, it's a wonderful tonic.

From the picnic tables, follow the Company Mill Trail (orange squares) over two rolling hills and come to Crabtree Creek. Cross the creek and turn right to walk to the remains of the Company Mill, which was built by the Page family in the early 1800s and used by the Cedar Rock community until the 1920s, when a flood destroyed it. The grinding stone for the gristmill is visible beside the trail.

KEY AT-A-GLANCE INFORMATION
Length:
9.5 miles
Configuration:
A balloon turned into a figure 8.
Difficulty:
Moderate due to length
Scenery:
Creeks, bluffs, old mill remains
Exposure:
Shady
Solitude:
Company Mill is often used by cross-country runners.
Trail surface:
Dirt, roots, rocks
Hiking time:
3.5 hours
Access:
No fees or permits
Maps:
State Park maps
Facilities:
Rest rooms, water, and picnic tables on both side of the park
Special comments:
This hike combines the 4.5-mile Company Mill Trail and the 5-mile Sycamore Loop.

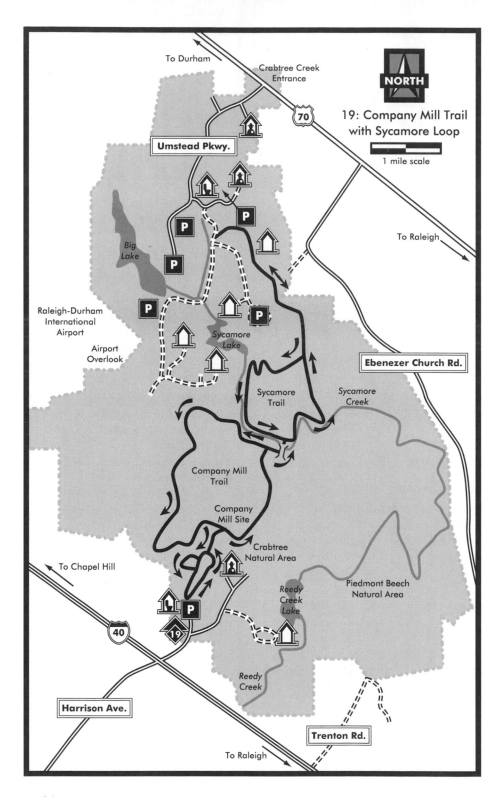

NORTH

19: Company Mill Trail
with Sycamore Loop

1 mile scale

To Durham

Crabtree Creek
Entrance

70

Umstead Pkwy.

To Raleigh

P

P

Big
Lake

P

Raleigh-Durham
International
Airport

P

Sycamore Lake

Airport
Overlook

P

Ebenezer Church Rd.

Sycamore
Trail

Sycamore
Creek

Company Mill
Trail

Company
Mill Site

Crabtree
Natural Area

To Chapel Hill

Reedy
Creek
Lake

Piedmont Beech
Natural Area

40

P

19

Reedy
Creek

Harrison Ave.

Trenton Rd.

To Raleigh

Remains of the Company Mill.

After leaving the mill, walk through a mixed hardwood forest until you reach a gravel road. The trail re-enters the woods about 40 yards to the right. After walking through the woods, you'll come to a station pointing out damage done to the pine trees by the southern pine beetle and a sign pointing you to the Sycamore Loop (blue triangles). To access the 3.5 miles on the Sycamore Loop, turn right and walk about 15 yards to a second gravel road. Cross the stone bridge and turn right to re-enter the woods.

For a short distance, the trail follows Sycamore Creek before it turns away from the creek and ascends a somewhat steep incline. Soon you'll come to a rail fence. Steep bluffs are on the left of the fence; you can walk on this side to peer down the rocky bluffs, but be careful.

Upon leaving the bluff, the trail crosses another gravel road. Re-enter the woods and continue walking until you come to the top of the Sycamore Loop.

Turn sharply to the right to begin your walk back to the Company Mill Trail. The trail to your left is the 1.5-mile stem of the Sycamore Loop that goes to the picnic area. If you include this out-and-back hike, you'll add another 3 miles to your total.

The second half of the Sycamore Loop is easy walking, and eventually you'll rejoin Sycamore Creek. Once again you'll come to the stone bridge. To rejoin the Company Mill Trail, walk to the left on the gravel road, and re-enter the woods. When you see the orange squares marking the Company Mill Trail, turn right. It's about three miles back to the parking lot.

If you want to get creative with this hike, you can. Where the footpaths cross the gravel roads, the rangers have posted laminated maps. You can shorten the mileage by walking along the gravel roads that dissect both the Company Mill Trail and the Sycamore Loop.

Cox Mountain Trail

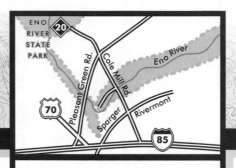

IN BRIEF

This hike is moderately challenging. If you hike during the winter when the trees are bare, good long-range views of up to 30 miles are possible. If you can't scare up the time to drive westward to the Pisgah or Nantahala National Forest, go here to satisfy your need for long-distance vistas.

DIRECTIONS

From Durham, travel west on Interstate 85. Exit onto US 70 West. Almost immediately, turn right onto Pleasant Green Road. Turn left onto Cole Mill Road; follow it until it ends in Eno River State Park. The Cox Mountain Trail, blazed blue, leaves from the parking lot.

DESCRIPTION

Cox Mountain has been described as the king of trails in the Eno River State Park. It is one of several trails in the Few's Ford area of the park. You'll cross two moderate peaks, one at 700 feet, the other at 688 feet.

After passing through the picnic area, the Cox Mountain Trail descends sharply to the river and then crosses a suspension bridge. Be sure not to hurry over the bridge; you'll miss a good view of the Eno. A spur to the left after the bridge leads to a park-provided cabin. Be sure to step over there, not so much to see the cabin as to see the high river

KEY AT-A-GLANCE INFORMATION

Length:
3.75 miles

Configuration:
Balloon

Difficulty:
Moderately challenging

Scenery:
30-mile views late fall to mid-spring

Exposure:
Shady

Solitude:
Moderate

Trail surface:
Dirt, not very root-bound or rocky

Hiking time:
Two hours

Access:
No fees or permits

Maps:
Eno River State Park, Few's Ford Section

Facilities:
Rest rooms and water are located in the park office before you reach the trailhead.

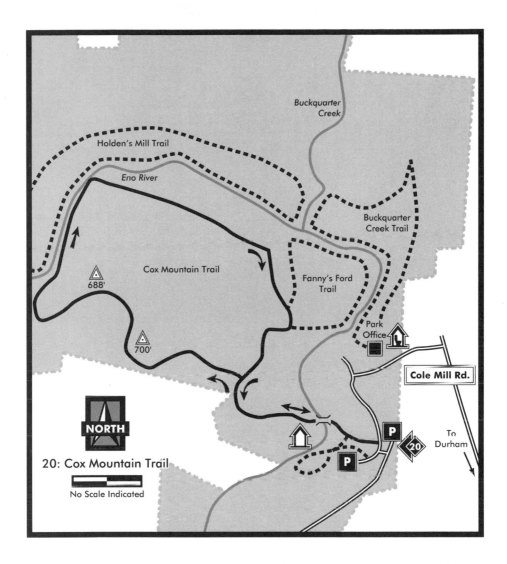

Buckquarter
Creek

Holden's Mill Trail

Eno River

Cox Mountain Trail

688'

700'

Buckquarter
Creek Trail

Fanny's Ford
Trail

Park
Office

Cole Mill Rd.

NORTH

20: Cox Mountain Trail

No Scale Indicated

P

P

20

To
Durham

bluffs covered with Catawba rhododendron and mountain laurel.

After rejoining the Cox Mountain
Trail, you'll walk along an old roadbed.
Soon you'll see the turn to climb the
nearly 700-foot high Cox Mountain. As
you traverse this mountain, be sure to
notice the variety of oak trees: white,
post, and red.

On the backside of Cox Mountain,
the trail is studded with white quartz. As
you quickly descend to river level, be
sure to look for the ferns and running

cedar that cover this wetter side of Cox
Mountain. The terrain looks very much
like that found in the Blue Ridge. As
you hike along the river, look for the
remnants of a dam.

Eventually, the Cox Mountain Trail
intersects Fanny's Ford Trail. You can go
left onto Fanny's Ford if you want to see
more of the Eno, or turn right to go
back to the parking lot. A trail off of
Fanny's Ford leads to a family camping
area. There are five sites with tent pads. A
pit toilet is located here. Fires are not

Bridge across the Eno River on the Cox Mountain Trail.

permitted, but camp stoves may be used. Camping permits are available at the park office for a small fee. Call (919) 383–1686 for information.

Of course, if you're really starved for mountain hiking, one more turn up and over Cox Mountain ought to cure your need for aerobic activity.

Crowder District Park Perimeter and Pond Trails

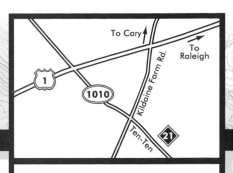

IN BRIEF

Located in a Wake County park that's chock-full of kid things, this trail is perfect for youngster, oldsters and everyone in between. During the spring, particularly March, the park is inundated with the sound of frogs, so much so that the park holds an annual Frog Festival.

DIRECTIONS

From Raleigh, take US 1 South and exit onto Ten-Ten Road (a.k.a. 1010). Drive south toward Fuquay-Varina. Crowder District Park is 4.2 miles on the left. From Cary, the park is 1.8 miles from the intersection of Kildaire Farm Road and NC 1010.

DESCRIPTION

Crowder District Park, the result of a 33-acre gift from Mrs. Doris P. Crowder in memory of her parents, contains two trails that can be combined for a good hike.

Birds spotted recently in the park by zoology students from nearby North Carolina State University include the red-bellied woodpecker, the American goldfinch, the hermit thrush, and bluebirds.

Crowder District Park is one of four Wake County parks, which circle around Raleigh. Crowder is located to the south of Raleigh. Lake Crabtree County Park is located to the west off of Interstate 40. Blue Jay Point County Park is located to

KEY AT-A-GLANCE INFORMATION

Length:
1.4 miles

Configuration:
Loop

Difficulty:
Easy

Scenery:
Crowder Pond

Exposure:
Part sun/part shade

Solitude:
Busy

Trail surface:
Asphalt

Hiking time:
15 minutes

Access:
No fees or permits

Maps:
Crowder District Park Map, provided by Wake County Parks

Facilities:
Rest rooms, water, open playground, tot lot with slides and swings

Special comments:
The Perimeter Trail 0.8 mile; the Pond Trail is 0.6 mile.

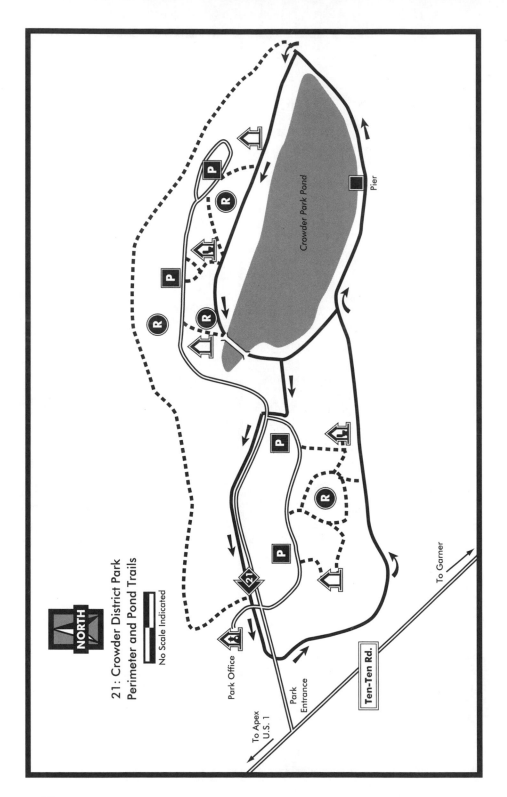

21: Crowder District Park
Perimeter and Pond Trails

NORTH

No Scale Indicated

Crowder Park Pond

Pier

Park Office

To Apex
U.S. 1

Park
Entrance

Ten-Ten Rd.

To Garner

the north off of Six Forks Road. Historic Oak View County Park is located to the east on Poole Road.

Begin on the Perimeter Trail (my name for the trail, since none currently exists) and hike to the right of the park office. The trail circles the edge of the park. As you descend a small hill, continue right along the perimeter and pass a small fishing pier. Shortly after passing the pier, you'll see another turn to the left to hike around the 2.7-acre pond. Take it and circle the pond.

If it's an early spring day or a warm evening, listen for the frogs. You may hear chorus frogs, spring peepers, bullfrogs, green frogs, and American toads. After circling the pond, you'll return to the Perimeter Trail. Take it to return to the park office.

Part of a master plan of parks development through the year 2010, Crowder District Park is helping to meet the needs of a Wake County population which doubled between the years 1980 and 2000, from approximately 300,000 to 600,000. By the year 2010, Wake will surpass Mecklenburg as the most populous county in North Carolina. Much of this growth has been attracted by the development of the Research Triangle area; Wake County houses over 50% of the population of the Research Triangle.

The park is open seven days a week, from 8 a.m. to sunset, except for major holidays. Call ahead for information on any special events that the park may be hosting at (919) 662-2850.

NEARBY ACTIVITIES

For a bite to eat after exploring the park, head back north on US 1 toward Raleigh. Turn left onto Walnut Street, and head east for a fast-food bazaar including Dairy Queen Brazier, 631 Walnut Street, (919) 460-1545). For less fried food, try Great Wraps, 1105 Walnut Street, (919) 380-9302).

Duke Cross-Country Trail

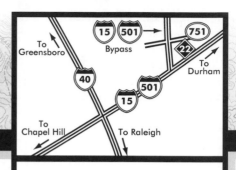

IN BRIEF

This enormously popular hike circles Duke University Golf Club. With the exception of one wicked hill—I'm not using the word wicked lightly, trust me—it's a moderately easy hike. Don't worry that you'll be hit by flying golf balls: The trail is thickly lined with trees.

DIRECTIONS

From the intersection of Interstate 40 and US 15/501 between Durham and Chapel Hill, drive north along US 15/501 Bypass to Durham. Exit onto NC 751, which is also known as Cameron Boulevard. The parking area is tucked just off Cameron Boulevard on the left, past the stoplight where Erwin Road begins.

DESCRIPTION

This prestigious course was beautifully designed by Robert Trent Jones. If walking around the golf course is a lesson in beauty, then the course itself, with fairways guarded by stately oaks and pines, is a touch of heaven. Envisioned in the early 1930s, course construction was halted in 1941 following the bombing of Pearl Harbor on December 7. After the war, construction plans were revived and the present 120-acre site was chosen.

Opened in 1957, the Duke Golf Club attracted its first NCAA men's championship in 1962. By 1988, the course was well worn and in need of a major facelift. For the redesign and restoration of

KEY AT-A-GLANCE INFORMATION

Length:
2.9 miles

Configuration:
Loop; the Fitness Trail adds a balloon.

Difficulty:
Easy

Scenery:
Urban forest, view of the Duke University Golf Course

Exposure:
Mostly shady

Solitude:
None

Trail surface:
Pine needles, gravel

Hiking time:
45 minutes

Access:
No fees or permits required

Maps:
None available

Facilities:
None

Special comments:
Add in the 0.6-mile Fitness Loop to bring the total to 3.7 miles.

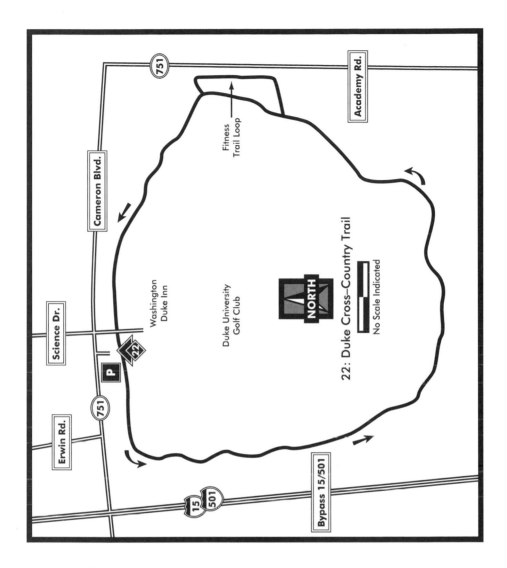

the course, Duke chose Rees Jones, the son of Robert Trent Jones. The makeover was completed in 1994.

Around 30 years ago, the Duke cross-country team actually trained on the golf course. Track Coach Al Buehler led the way to build the nearly three-mile path around the course. In the spring of 2000, Buehler stepped down after serving for 45 years as head coach of the men's track and cross-country teams. In his honor, the cross-country trail was renamed the Al Buehler Trail. In addition to cross-country runners and hikers from the area, Buehler himself runs the loop five days a week. Whenever you walk this trail, you're going to see people—lots of them. But for all of the wear and tear this trail receives, it's in good shape.

From the parking area, just start walking. If you hike to the right, you'll get to climb the hill. It's a long, steady pull, so just put it in goat-gear and go. When you get to the top, you can stop to enjoy the view down the golf course while your breathing returns to normal. Along the way, you'll hear road noise from the US 15/501 Bypass, and you'll probably see golfers lining up their shots.

If you want to add in the 0.6-mile Fitness Loop, look for a spur to the right after ascending the big hill. (If you hiked left from the parking lot, the Fitness Loop is the second spur to your left.) This trail goes down to Duke University Road and then circles back to the Cross-Country Trail. Along the way, you can stop in at one or all of the 32 fitness stations.

Durham Pump Station

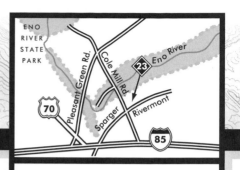

IN BRIEF

This pleasant hike in Eno River State Park passes the remnants of five buildings related to the Durham Pump Station, which was built in 1887. Although many of the trails in Eno River State Park are good for viewing spring wildflowers, rangers think this is one of the best, especially in late March and early April.

DIRECTIONS

From Durham: Travel Interstate 85 west and exit onto Cole Mill Road. Turn right on Rivermont Road. Rivermont Road becomes a gravel road. The Pump Station Trailhead is just left after the bridge. Parking consists of widened pullouts on either side of the bridge.

DESCRIPTION

In the late 1800s, Durham was growing. But the town, depending on municipal ponds for water, lacked sufficient infrastructure to support continued growth. Plus, during the 1870s and 1880s, the city suffered several fires, and many of the businesses found it difficult to purchase insurance.

To solve the problems, Durham contracted with a Boston firm in 1886 to build a water system. A grand plan was conceived: A 100-foot dam would cross the Eno, holding 6 million gallons of water. A storage basin, some 8,300 feet away, would hold 3.5 million gallons of water. During the heyday of the reser-

KEY AT-A-GLANCE INFORMATION

Length:
1.5 miles

Configuration:
Loop

Difficulty:
Easy

Scenery:
Remains of turn-of-the-century industrial buildings

Exposure:
Shady

Solitude:
Moderate

Trail surface:
Dirt, gravel

Hiking time:
30 minutes

Access:
No fees or permits

Maps:
Eno River State Park

Facilities:
None

Special comments:
Avoid walking on the ruins of the Pump Station to protect the structure.

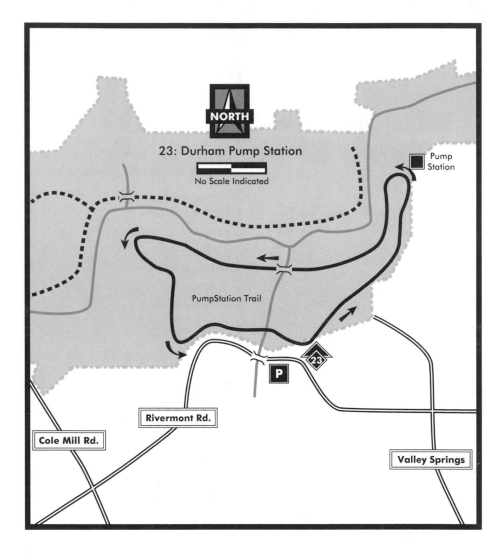

23: Durham Pump Station

No Scale Indicated

Pump
Station

PumpStation Trail

23

P

Rivermont Rd.

Cole Mill Rd.

Valley Springs

voir, bathhouses encouraged swimmers and the Red Cross often conducted swimming lessons. Soon, though, Durham outgrew the capacity and opted to build a new reservoir north of the city. The new reservoir was named Lake Michie, in honor of J.C. Michie, who managed the original Durham Pump Station.

Because the city of Durham often looked to the Eno River as a source of water, the Eno River Association, led by Margaret and Holger Nygard, organized in 1965 to protect and preserve the Eno River Valley. The legacy of their work is that today the Eno River is a "free-flowing, clean stream in an urban setting." Although development on the Eno in the past, such as the Durham Pump Station, went relatively unchallenged, today the Eno River and its protected green areas has friends who guard against further exploitation. The river and its parks and trails effectively serve as a "green buffer against continuing urban sprawl" and its demands.

Eno River State Park, along with its smaller city park neighbor—West Point on the Eno—together encompass more than 2,630 acres of public recreation. Despite the human demands placed on the Eno in recent history, its water remains relatively clean and is home to beavers, otters and over 60 species of fish. In the eighteenth and nineteenth centuries as many as 52 grain mills ground corn and wheat using the Eno's flow of energy. The parks, along with the Eno River Association, work hard to protect and maintain the Eno and attractions such as the Pump Station Trail.

Following the trail from the parking area through a mixed-wood forest, you'll come to the brick foundation of the station and a large fireplace on the right. Farther on, you'll see the actual pump-house and its sluice channels. (The other buildings were situated behind the fireplace.)

After passing the Pump Station, the trail follows the river a short distance. It eventually swings away from the river, turning left onto an old roadbed. You'll know you're near the end when you see the roadbed continuing to the right and a trail leading to the left through some pine trees.

One of several gnawed stumps, indicating beaver activity in Eno River State Park.

Staying on the roadbed brings you to Rivermont Road, out of eyeshot of the parking area at the bridge. (The bridge is down the hill to your left.) Take the trail to the left through the pine trees to return directly to the bridge and parking area.

Eno River Trail, North and South

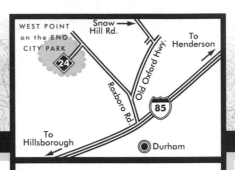

WEST POINT on the ENO CITY PARK 24

Snow Hill Rd. →

To Henderson →

Roxboro Rd.

Old Oxford Hwy.

85

To Hillsborough

⊙ Durham

IN BRIEF

These two trails, located in Durham's favorite city park, West Point on the Eno, parallel the Eno River through the park to Guess Road. You can walk them both as a loop or either side as an out-and-back hike. You'll be amazed at the remote feel of this hike when you reach the mid-point of either of the two trails.

DIRECTIONS

West Point on the Eno is located on the left on Roxboro Road in Durham, about four miles north of Interstate 85.

DESCRIPTION

Though now a city park, this area is actually older than the city of Durham. Located along a two-mile stretch of the Eno River, the area was once home to Native Americans such as the Eno, Shocco, and Occaneechi.

The community even saw a little bit of upheaval after the Civil War. Union General William T. Sherman stationed his cavalry here while he conducted sur-render negotiations at nearby Bennett Place with Confederate General Joseph E. Johnston.

The south-side trail departs from the McCown Mill—located below the McCown-Mangum House—through the picnic area, just after you cross a concrete-and-stone, low-water dam at the mill. The mill functioned until 1942, when a storm damaged it. But the water-powered grist-

KEY AT-A-GLANCE INFORMATION

Length:
3.4 miles
Configuration:
Out-and-back
Difficulty:
Easy
Scenery:
Tall river bluffs, mixed-wood forests
Exposure:
Shady
Solitude:
Remote, once you leave the center of the park
Trail surface:
Dirt
Hiking time:
1.5 hours
Access:
No fees or permits
Maps:
Map is on a wooden sign located near the mill.
Facilities:
Rest rooms can be found at the McCown-Mangum House
Special comments:
Two trails run the length of the river, and both are 1.7 miles long. If you hike here, step inside the Mangum Museum of Photography. Be aware, too, that this park is where the Fourth of July Festival for the Eno is held.

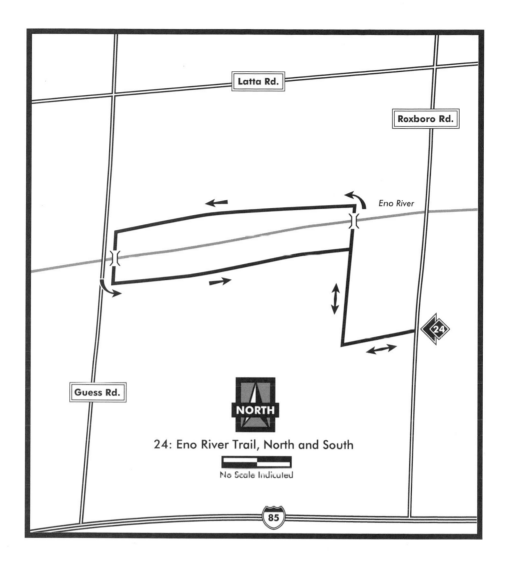

Latta Rd.

Roxboro Rd.

Eno River

Guess Rd.

NORTH

24: Eno River Trail, North and South

No Scale Indicated

24

85

mill was rebuilt and is still operational today.

Both trails dead-end at Guess Road. If you first hike the north side, cross the bridge and look for a trail just past the bridge. Be careful at the end of the south side trail; the culvert is full of trash and, possibly, broken bottles. If you hiked the south-side first, cross the bridge and look for an old roadbed that goes behind the private residence.

The footpath is mostly obvious, which is good, since the trails are not blazed and

likely to be overgrown with honeysuckle in the warm months. You will, however, see the occasional wooden bench that assures you that you haven't wandered into the state park portion of the Eno River. Regardless of which side you hike first, you'll enjoy the feeling that you're far from the desk and no longer in an urban area.

The park is open year-round from 8 a.m. until dusk. Call ahead for the working hours of the historic buildings at (919) 471-1623.

NEARBY ACTIVITIES

Embarking at West Point on the Eno, guided river trips in inflatable kayaks have become a popular activity. Known as "wafting" expeditions, thousands of paddlers have indulged in this slow-paced river travel. "River Dave," the resident field naturalist at West Point on the Eno, leads wafting trips, including trips by moonlight where Dave teaches wafters listening to a soothing drum beat how to meditate while floating down the Eno. Contact the park at (919) 471-1623 for more information.

Fallon Creek Trail

IN BRIEF

This short, easy trail, part of the Raleigh Greenway system, is notable for the former champion river birch tree that stands nearby. You'll have to see this tree to believe just how large a river birch can grow. Be on the lookout, too, for some beautiful sycamore trees. You'll know them by their scaly white trunks.

DIRECTIONS

Fallon Creek Trail links Oxford Road to Kiwanis Park, which is on Noble Road. (Noble Road intersects Wake Forest Road close to Southern States Nissan.) You can park anywhere on Oxford Road behind Our Lady of Lourdes Elementary School (on the hill where Anderson Drive intersects Oxford Road) or at Kiwanis Park.

DESCRIPTION

The Fallon Creek Trail will one day be part of the completed Crabtree Creek Greenway. Walking along the Fallon Creek Trail, you'll see the famous Crabtree Creek—a creek that seems to always flood during periods of heavy rain and causes the car dealerships located on Wake Forest Road to move their cars to higher ground. To appreciate just how high the water can be here, look for the hand railings leading down to Oxford Road from Our Lady of Lourdes Church, near the entrance to the path.

KEY AT-A-GLANCE INFORMATION

Length:
1 mile

Configuration:
Out-and-back

Difficulty:
Easy

Scenery:
Crabtree Creek meanders nearby on the left.

Exposure:
Shady

Solitude:
Busy mornings when people are running; also busy on weekends with cyclists

Trail surface:
Paved

Hiking time:
12 minutes

Access:
No fees or permits

Maps:
Capital Area Greenway Trail System or Raleigh Bike Map

Facilities:
Rest rooms, water, ballfields, and picnic shelter at Kiwanis Park

Special comments:
Like many of the paved greenways, this trail is wheelchair-traversible.

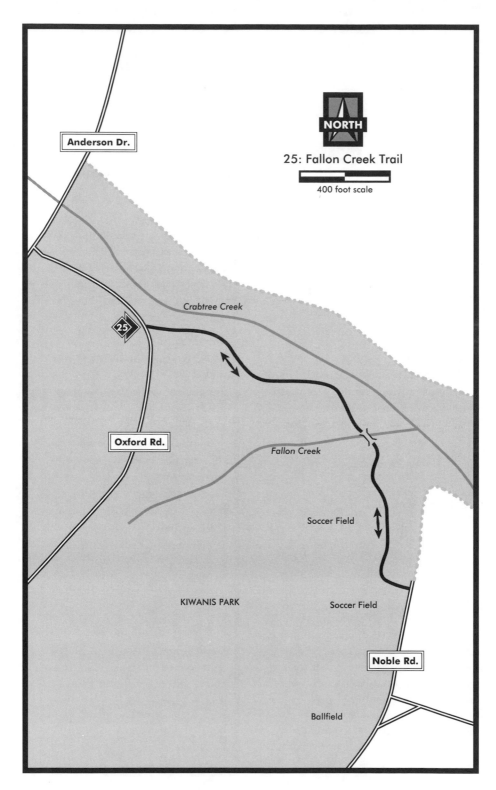

NORTH

25: Fallon Creek Trail

400 foot scale

Anderson Dr.

Crabtree Creek

25

Oxford Rd.

Fallon Creek

Soccer Field

KIWANIS PARK

Soccer Field

Noble Rd.

Ballfield

Hurricanes Fran and Floyd caused water to rise to the top of the bottom railing!

The larger Crabtree Creek, which intersects Fallon Creek, not only floods but is also a point of concern with residents concerned over the health of the Neuse River. During heavy rains, Crabtree Creek empties a muddy plume into the Neuse. Development in the Crabtree Creek watershed has been blamed for the heavy sediment output of the creek.

Visiting the Fallon Creek Trail is worth the walk to see a former champion river birch tree. In 1991, this big tree was the largest river birch tree in the area, as determined by the NCSU School of Forestry. Since then, however, the tree has been superseded by an even larger river birch that's located on the Neuse River near the Buffalo Road Canoe Launch.

Heading south, a small bridge will lead you across Fallon Creek. Here, the trail leads out from the floodplain forest to an open area. The trail ends at Noble Road, the turnaround for the short hike back.

This trail is great for kids. The short distance and zigzag nature of the path should be able to capture the shortest of attention spans. Bikes and Big Wheels are allowed. Hikers may also have to share the greenway with in-line skaters. The smooth asphalt is ideal for their small wheels.

After you hike this trail, you might enjoy spending time in nearby Fallon Park, which is to the left up Oxford Road, especially if you're out with your dog. Your pets will enjoy the extra exercise through the park on the many casual trails.

Falls Lake Trail

Pleasant Union Church Rd.

26

Entrance to
Blue Jay Point Park

Possum Track Rd.

Six Forks Rd.

To Raleigh

IN BRIEF

Want to test your rock-skipping skills? If so, hike this triangle of a footpath that traverses the rolling hillside along Falls Lake. There's enough distance—and pebbles—out here to try for a five- or six-skipper. You could spend all day out there working on your pitching arm!

DIRECTIONS

Blue Jay Point Park is located within the Falls Lake State Recreation Area. Located 10 miles north of Raleigh and 12 miles east of Durham, the lake and woodlands combine for 36,000 acres of outdoor fun. Blue Jay Point Park is located on Pleasant Union Church Road, north of the Bayleaf community off of Six Forks Road. The Falls Lake Trail can be accessed from Blue Jay Point Trail, which leaves from the circle on the entrance road.

DESCRIPTION

This trail, since it is part of the Mountains-to-the-Sea Trail, is blazed with a white circle.

There are lots of hardwoods to pass under and creeks to jump along this trail. You'll also find lots of benches if you want a quiet place just to watch the sun reflect off the water. Look for mountain laurel on north-facing slopes. Although the boat traffic can be noisy, you'll find that no trail in the Triangle delivers as many fine lake views.

KEY AT-A-GLANCE INFORMATION

Length:
6.2 miles
Configuration:
Out-and-back
Difficulty:
Moderate
Scenery:
Falls Lake, hardwood trees
Exposure:
Filtered sun
Solitude:
Boat noise in the summer
Trail surface:
Dirt, pine needles, leaves
Hiking time:
3 hours
Access:
No fees or permits
Maps:
Falls Lake Map, available at the U.S. Army Corps Management Center and Dam
Facilities:
Rest rooms, water, picnic tables, environmental education programs, kid-friendly playgrounds, fishing with NC freshwater license
Special comments:
Be aware that the name Falls Lake Trail refers to six sections of trail that follow Falls Lake. Section IV, described here, is located in Blue Jay Point Park. It's the best one to walk.

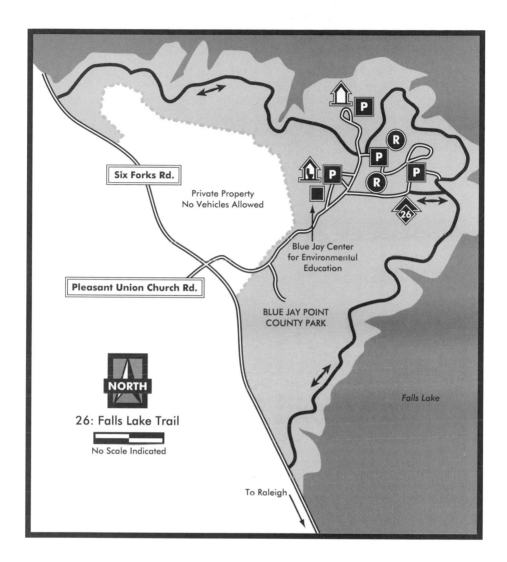

Six Forks Rd.

Private Property
No Vehicles Allowed

Blue Jay Center
for Environmental
Education

Pleasant Union Church Rd.

BLUE JAY POINT
COUNTY PARK

NORTH

26: Falls Lake Trail

No Scale Indicated

Falls Lake

To Raleigh

When you finish hiking, step inside the Blue Jay Environmental Center to see the exhibits explaining the cycle water follows from raindrop to drinking water. You're sure to come away with a better appreciation of how the Neuse River Basin, the Falls Lake watershed, and the local citizenry are interconnected. The park is open 8 a.m. to sunset, seven days a week, except Thanksgiving Day, Christmas Eve and Day, and New Year's Day. Call the park at (919) 870-4330 for more information.

If you decide you're up for the whole enchilada and want to hike the entire 23 miles of the Falls Lake Trail, the western trailhead is located near the park office on NC 50. You can also go to Falls Lake Dam, located north of Raleigh on Falls of Neuse Road, to access the trail from the east.

NEARBY ACTIVITIES
With a recreation area this large, there are plenty of activities to pursue. A short drive away, nearby Shinleaf Recreation

Area contains another two miles of the Mountains-to-the-Sea Trail. To reach Shinleaf from Blue Jay Point Park, turn right onto Six Forks Road and look for signs directing you to the area. There are picnic areas here as well as at Blue Jay Point. For drinks and snacks on the lake, head to Rolling View Marina. Take Six Forks Road back to Highway 98, which you'll cross on the way to Shinleaf, and turn right, headed southwest. Turn right on Baptist Road, which will lead you to the marina.

In addition to a snack bar, the marina offers boat-launching facilities, fishing, rest rooms, a washhouse, swimming, camping, and equipment rental. Call the park office at (919) 676-1027 for more information on Rolling View Marina.

Fanny's Ford

IN BRIEF

Named for African-American midwife, Fanny Breeze, who lived and ministered in the area after the Civil War, this easy walk in the Few's Ford section of Eno River State Park provides great views of the river, passes by remnants of a grist-mill built in 1758, and follows for a short distance a roadbed dating back to colonial days.

DIRECTIONS

From Durham, travel west on Interstate 85. Exit onto US 70 West. Almost immediately, turn right onto Pleasant Green Road. Turn left onto Cole Mill Road and follow it until it ends in the Few's Ford Access section of Eno River State Park. Park in the second parking area.

DESCRIPTION

From the second parking area, follow the blue blazes of the Cox Mountain Trail until you see the purple-blazed Fanny's Ford Trail.

Hiked clockwise, this easy riverside walk goes down to the river by first passing through an area thick with running cedar and sweet gum trees. It then circles a primitive camping area and passes by a spot in the river crowded with huge lichen-covered boulders. As you circle the area, look across the river and up the hill: This is where Fanny lived. The churchyard where Fanny is buried, along

KEY AT-A-GLANCE INFORMATION

Length:
1 mile

Configuration:
Balloon

Difficulty:
Moderate

Scenery:
River views

Exposure:
Shady

Solitude:
Busy

Trail surface:
Dirt

Hiking time:
30 minutes

Access:
No fees or permits

Maps:
Eno River State Park, Few's Ford section

Facilities:
Rest rooms and water are located at the park office on the way in. Only picnic tables are located near this trailhead.

Special comments:
You can easily combine this with the Buckquarter Creek hike and the Cox Mountain Trail hike.

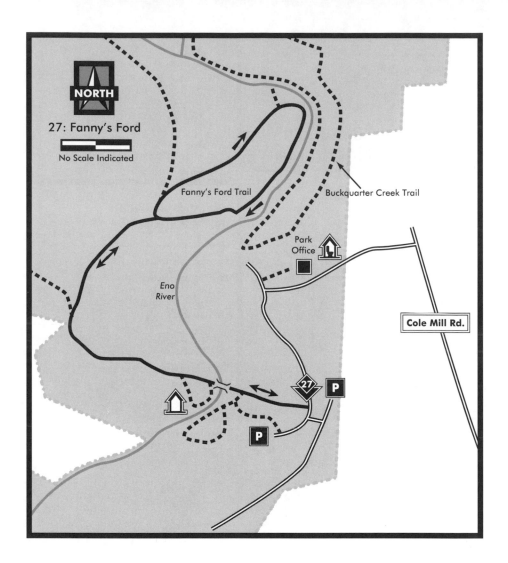

with her husband and daughter, is less than a mile away up and over the hill as the crow flies.

Speaking of crows, bird watching is a favorite activity of visitors to this area. Approximately 152 species of birds have been spotted in the park. In the spring, prairie warblers, indigo buntings, and blue grosbeaks sing for their nesting territories. In the summer, look for brown thrashers and mockingbirds. During winter, flocks of cedar waxwings descend to feed on cedar berries.

The family camping area is accessed off of Fanny's Ford Trail. There are five tent sites. A pit toilet is located here for campers and hikers. Obtain camping permits at the park office. No fires are allowed, but camp stoves may be used.

The trail follows the Eno River upstream, passing Few's Ford and the remnants of Few's Mill. Notice the old roadbed you hike on after turning away from the river, past the ford. This is a remnant of the old Hillsborough Coach Road.

NEARBY ACTIVITIES

The town of Hillsborough, located at the junction of Interstates 40 and 85, is less than 10 miles from Eno River State Park. First occupied by Native Americans, colonists settled here in the mid-1700s. Hillsborough is named after William Hill, Earl of Hillsborough. Hill served as Secretary of State for the Colonies from 1768 through 1772 under England's King George III.

The draw of modern Hillsborough remains its ties to the colonial past. The historic town contains over 100 late eighteenth- and early nineteenth-century buildings. In Hillsborough, your first stop should be the visitor's center located near the corner of Margaret Lane and Court Street, across from the Old Orange County Courthouse. Sights of interest are numerous, including the visitor's center, which is a restored home.

Fish Traps Trail

IN BRIEF

Named for the fish baskets Native Americans once used to catch fish, this easy trail in Raven Rock State Park leads to a spot on the Cape Fear River where you can see the remains of Northington's Lock and Dam. The trail is short but has steep climbs near the river.

DIRECTIONS

From Raleigh: Travel south on US 401 to Lillington. At the intersection of US 421 and US 401 in downtown Lillington, turn right onto US 421 North. Follow the signs to Raven Rock State Park. Trails begin from the left, center, and right of the parking lot.

DESCRIPTION

From the parking lot, take the Northington Ferry Trail (center), continuing past the Raven Rock Loop Trail, which you'll see on your right. Shortly after this trail, look for Fish Traps Trail to peel away to the right off of Northington Ferry Trail. The Fish Traps Trail descends, at first gently and then steeply, to lock and dam remains. The locks and dam were built by the Cape Fear and Deep River Navigation Company in the early 1850s to help steamboats paddle upstream. A hurricane roared through in 1859, sweeping away the locks and parts of the dam. The structure was never rebuilt.

Though it's hard to believe today, the Cape Fear River was once quite busy

KEY AT-A-GLANCE INFORMATION

Length:
1.1 miles

Configuration:
Out-and-back

Difficulty:
Easy

Scenery:
Cape Fear River, remains of locks and dams

Exposure:
Shady

Solitude:
Busy on weekends

Trail surface:
Sandy and rock-strewn

Hiking time:
30 minutes

Access:
No fees or permits

Maps:
Raven Rock State Park

Facilities:
Rest rooms, water, picnic tables, snack machines

Special comments:
You can easily combine this with the American Beech Trail. (Campbell Creek Trail is on the other side of the park.)

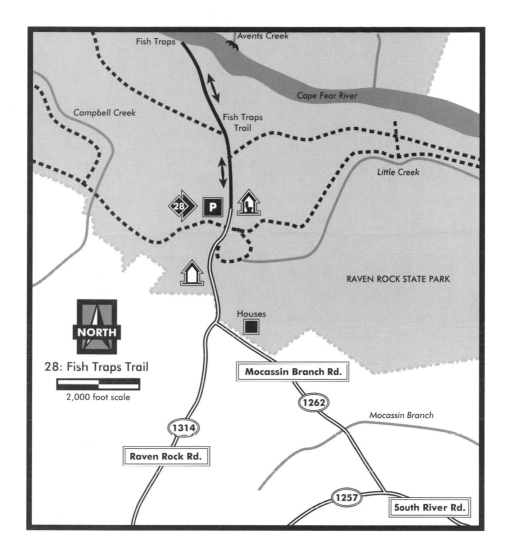

NORTH

28: Fish Traps Trail

2,000 foot scale

with paddleboats, the kind that traveled up and down the Mississippi River.

As you hike along the trail, look for a series of white quartzite boulders on the right that resemble jagged teeth. These boulders indicate that you're hiking through the fall line, a geological line distinguishing the softer sedimentary rocks of the coastal plain from the harder rocks of the Piedmont. Quartz formations in Raven Rock State Park are thought to be about 450 million years old. Quartz was used by area Native

Americans to fashion tools, including arrow points, drills, and scrapers.

This trail is popular with folks who like to fish the Cape Fear River, since it provides relatively quick and easy access to the water. When you see the smooth rock ledges down at river level, you'll understand why Native Americans would place their fish-trapping baskets here. Settlers learned from the native people the importance of fish as a food and often staked out land claims based on whether or not the land contained a good site for

Remains of a dam on the Cape Fear River.

a fish trap. Two types of fish traps were used by the native people: the basket trap and the weir. The weir consisted of V-shaped rock structures built in the river or creek. Swimming downstream the fish would funnel together into the V, where they were speared.

Although short, the Fish Traps Trail is a worthy venture and provides a quick route to the Cape Fear River. It's also not as busy as the Raven Rock Loop. As you approach the river, forest noises will gradually yield to the roar of the Cape Fear rapids. In August and September,

watch carefully as you hike to avoid stepping on tiny baby frogs making their initial foray onto solid ground.

If you like to fish, the trail's turn-around at the Cape Fear is an excellent spot to cast for largemouth bass, bluegill, or catfish. If you don't want to catch the fish and are patient, you may be able to see a few silvery leaps as you relax on the bank.

Hikers, especially in warm weather, have noted how humid the air feels near the Cape Fear River.

CLEMMONS EDUCATIONAL STATE FOREST

To Garner

Old US 70

70

29

To Goldsboro

Forest Demonstration and Forest Geology Trails

IN BRIEF
Talking rocks make this easy and educational hike through Clemmons Educational State Forest a joy. The hike emphasizes understanding the forest environment.

DIRECTIONS
From Raleigh: Drive east on US 70. Signs point the way to Clemmons Educational State Forest, which is about five miles south of Garner

DESCRIPTION
This is definitely a hike with a theme: forestry education. Planned trails such as the Forest Demonstration and Geology Trails provide hikers, especially children, with a focused learning experience. The forest trail teaches hikers about forest ecology, tree development and identification, and the impact of fire. The geology trail highlights landscape changes such as rock outcroppings or eroded areas and explains the significance of each.

The only difficult part of this hike is finding where to start. Once you've done that, you're good to go. At the parking lot, walk down any of the trails that weave in and out of the picnic area. As you do, make your way left to the Forest Center, which explains the many wood products produced by trees found in North Carolina. Here you'll find the trailhead for three trails: the red–blazed Forest Demonstration Trail (right), the yellow-

KEY AT-A-GLANCE INFORMATION

Length:
3 miles

Configuration:
Loop within a loop

Difficulty:
Easy

Scenery:
Forest management techniques

Exposure:
Often sunny, due to controlled burns and clearings

Solitude:
Can be busy

Trail surface:
Wood chips, gravel, dirt, sand, pine needles

Hiking time:
50 minutes

Access:
No fees or permits

Maps:
Available at the office on the way in. Trails are also noted on a board in the middle of the parking lot.

Facilities:
Rest rooms, water, picnic tables

Special comments:
This hike consists of two parts: 2.2 miles on the Forest Demonstration Trail and 0.8 mile on the Forest Geology Trail.

93

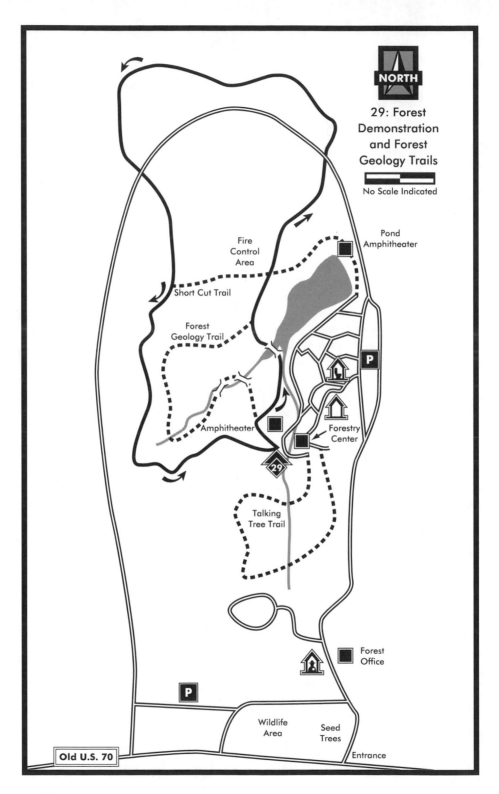

NORTH

29: Forest
Demonstration
and Forest
Geology Trails

No Scale Indicated

Pond
Amphitheater

Fire
Control
Area

Short Cut Trail

Forest
Geology Trail

Amphitheater

Forestry
Center

29

Talking
Tree Trail

Forest
Office

P

Wildlife
Area

Seed
Trees

Entrance

Old U.S. 70

blazed Forest Geology Trail (center), and the green-blazed Talking Tree Trail (left).

Turn right and begin walking the 2.2-mile Forest Demonstration Trail. This trail crosses over a pond and then climbs a gentle hill up an area where a controlled burn was held. A short-cut trail comes up on your left, but don't take it. Continue walking along to where the trail intersects a gravel service road. Turn left. The trail, though noted on maps as going straight across the road, no longer does so. Due to damage from Hurricane Floyd and a severe erosion problem, the trail is being rerouted.

After using the road to cross to the upper edge of the forest, you'll leave the road and once again enter the woods, where you'll pass the other side of the burned field. Continue following the trail until it returns to the Forest Center, where you can pick up the Forest Geology Trail. Be sure to listen to the rocks as they tell you about the forest soil. As you walk along these trails, try to imagine how this area appeared during the 1920s, when it was cleared and the land was used for growing cotton.

In addition to Clemmons, the North Carolina Division of Forest Resources operates a system of five other Educational State Forests. The forests exist to teach the public, especially schoolchildren, about the complexity and necessity of forest environments. Each forest contains self-guided trail tours. Rangers are available to conduct classes for school groups. The demonstration trails have become so popular with teachers, they must make reservations for their students months in advance. For more information call, (919) 553-5651.

NEARBY ACTIVITIES

If you're headed back to Raleigh on US 70 and you need to find a place to eat try A Place to Eat. That's the name: A Place to Eat. The restaurant is located in Garner, just south of Raleigh, at 1340 West Garner Road. The restaurant, which specializes in new Louisiana country-style cooking, serves breakfast, lunch, and dinner. Try one of the many blackened dishes such as steak, grouper, or salmon. Simpler dishes are available for kids. The phone number is (919) 779-6411.

Also, if you hike here in the spring, you may see lots of folks with strawberries for sale; in the fall, you may find people selling pecans.

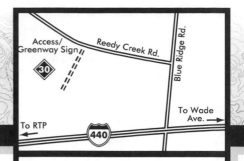

Frances L. Liles Trail

IN BRIEF

This walk passes through Schenck Forest, the research forest used by the School of Forest Resources at NCSU. Because it serves as an outdoor laboratory, take the kids to help them learn how to distinguish between various species of trees and to appreciate the merits of a controlled burn.

DIRECTIONS

From Raleigh: From Blue Ridge Road, near the North Carolina Museum of Art, turn left onto Reedy Creek Road. Travel Reedy Creek Road until the pavement turns to gravel. After passing several government buildings, you'll pass several NCSU agricultural stations. Look for a sign on the left marking the Carl A. Schenck Memorial Forest. Turn left onto another gravel road. The gate is on the right about 0.2 mile ahead. Park at the gate.

DESCRIPTION

Although you're near Interstate 40, the fairgrounds, and the Entertainment and Sports Arena, the nearby pastures and barns associated with North Carolina State University's School of Agriculture will make you think you're really out in the country when you hike here.

Carl A. Schenck Memorial Forest is named for the German forester employed by George Vanderbilt to manage the forests that were initially associated with

KEY AT-A-GLANCE INFORMATION

Length:
1.2 miles

Configuration:
Balloon

Difficulty:
Easy

Scenery:
Several patches where trees are planted in rows

Exposure:
Shady in the woods; sunny along the dirt road leading to the trailhead

Solitude:
None

Trail surface:
Dirt and roots in the woods; gravel along the road

Hiking time:
30 minutes

Access:
No fees or permits

Maps:
None available

Facilities:
Picnic table

Special comments:
No bikes are allowed and dogs must be kept on leashes.

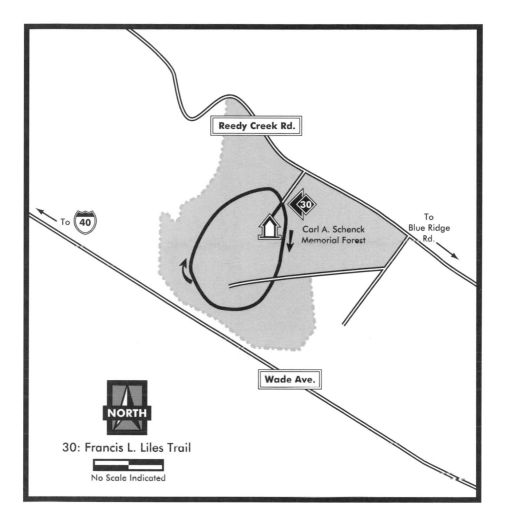

Reedy Creek Rd.

To **40**

30

Carl A. Schenck
Memorial Forest

To
Blue Ridge
Rd.

Wade Ave.

NORTH

30: Francis L. Liles Trail

No Scale Indicated

the Biltmore Estate. The trail itself is named for Frances L. Liles, the much-loved first administrative assistant for the NCSU School of Forest Resources.

Managed by NCSU, the 254-acre forest preserve functions as an outdoor laboratory for students at the university and as an outdoor refuge for Raleigh residents. Visitors can preview the trail by taking an online virtual field trip of the Schenck Forest at www.cfr.ncsu.edu/for/schenck/.

After parking at the gate, walk down the gravel road until you see a picnic area on the right. Turn toward the picnic

shelter, passing a memorial to Schenck that stands next to a huge oak tree (a friend of mine, Tracie, says it's a "kick-butt" oak tree, and she's right). The Frances L. Liles Trail, blazed in yellow, begins behind the picnic shelter.

At first the trail passes through a forest planted on what was farmland during the 1800s. Along the way, you'll cross a creek several times on wooden footbridges and you'll encounter interpretive stations pointing out various trees and how those trees are used. Note: The field that was badly damaged by Hurricane Fran; the sign indicates that the recovery period for the forest is estimated to be between 15 and 20 years. According to forest managers, it's a good place to see indigo buntings. As you near Reedy Creek, you'll see the remains of an old dam from the 1800s, proving that once the area was used not as a forest but as a farm.

You'll parallel Richland Creek on the lower portion of the trail. As you do, you'll probably notice the Loblolly Trail coming in below, to your right. At a junction marked by two trees painted with red and white stripes, hike left along what looks like an old roadbed. (If you take the connector trail to the right between the two trees painted with stripes, you'll go down a small hill and access the Loblolly Trail.)

Eventually, the roadbed leads through stands of pine trees, some of which have been subject to two-year forest management burns and others that have not.

The roadbed you're hiking upon intersects a gravel road. Turn left. At the end of the road, you will see the gate where you left the car. Once again you'll pass the

Tracie's "Kick-butt" oak tree near the Francis L. Liles Trail.

picnic table and the giant "kick-butt" oak tree.

Hemlock Bluffs Ramble

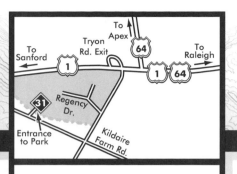

IN BRIEF

A little piece of heaven: That's what this trail passes through. The terrain and plant life—especially the Eastern Hemlocks—bear a striking resemblance to Linville Gorge, and the wildflowers that bloom here in the spring are not to be missed.

DIRECTIONS

From Raleigh: Drive to Cary on US 64 West/US 1 South. Take the Tryon Road exit where US 64 and US 1 split, south of Cary. Loop underneath the Beltline and travel to the intersection of Tryon and Kildaire Farm Roads. Turn right. Hemlock Bluffs is 1.4 miles on the right after you pass the Crossroads Crescent and Waverly Shopping Centers. The trails begin in front of the Stevens Nature Center.

DESCRIPTION

This little gem of a park has its origins in the last glacial period, some 10,000 years ago. Although Wake County wasn't covered with glaciers, it did experience much cooler temperatures due to the relatively close glaciers. But as the glaciers retreated due to a warming trend, all of the plant communities that thrived in the cooler temperatures also disappeared—all that is, except for the plants growing on the north side of the bluffs. Here the natural air conditioning of Swift Creek and the typically cooler temperatures found on north-facing

KEY AT-A-GLANCE INFORMATION

Length:
About 2 miles

Configuration:
Barbell

Difficulty:
Moderate

Scenery:
Hemlock trees and other plants typically found in the mountains

Exposure:
Shady

Solitude:
None

Trail surface:
Wood chips and dirt

Hiking time:
45 minutes

Access:
No fees or permits

Maps:
Hemlock Bluffs Nature Preserve Map provided by the Town of Cary Parks System

Facilities:
Rest rooms and water

Special comments:
This hike is composed of three trails: the Chestnut Oak Loop (1.1 miles), the Swift Creek Loop (0.6 mile), and the Beech Tree Cove Trail (0.3 mile).

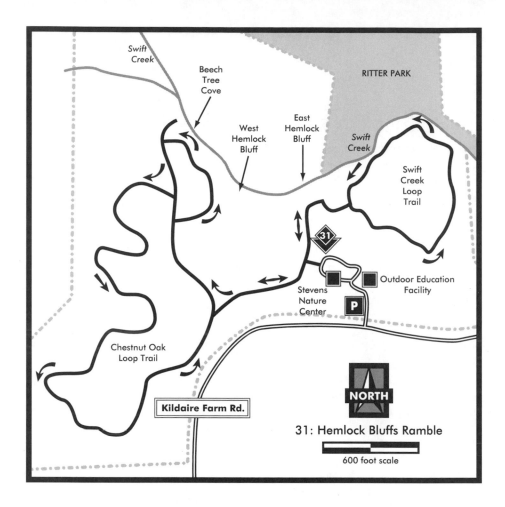

Swift
Creek

Beech
Tree
Cove

RITTER PARK

West
Hemlock
Bluff

East
Hemlock
Bluff

Swift
Creek

Swift
Creek
Loop
Trail

31

Outdoor Education
Facility

Stevens
Nature
Center

P

Chestnut Oak
Loop Trail

Kildaire Farm Rd.

NORTH

31: Hemlock Bluffs Ramble

600 foot scale

slopes caused the hemlock trees and wildflowers to stay. (Tracie, a hiking buddy, says it's very cool here in the summer and is one of the places where she seeks relief from the hot weather. She hangs her head over the platform at the bluffs to let the cool air rush over her face.) It is the only place in the state outside of the western mountains where hemlocks occur naturally.

To see this mountain beauty, begin at the Stevens Nature Center. Turn right on the trail and walk first to the East Hemlock Bluff. You can look out over the creek from several decks. Then hike down the stairs to access the 0.6-mile Swift Creek Loop. There you can see trilliums, violets, dwarf irises, and wild azaleas blooming during the spring, as well as running cedar. When you complete the Swift Creek Loop, climb up the stairs and walk to the Chestnut Oak Loop, which can be found on the other side of the bluffs.

When you reach the Chestnut Oak Loop (1.1 miles), bear right and go first to West Hemlock Bluff, where you'll have a nearly 360-degree view of the coves and bluffs. As you walk to the viewing platform, be sure to look over your right shoulder, back toward the slopes. The hemlock trees and steep slopes will fool you momentarily into thinking you're at Linville Gorge. After climbing down to

Eastern Hemlock viewing area at Hemlock Bluffs.

the viewing platform for the east side, climb up, walk to the right, and then climb down to Beech Cove.

After climbing up from Beech Cove, continue walking to the right along Chestnut Oak Trail. Soon you'll return to the Stevens Nature Center.

While you're there, stop in the nature center and sample one of their numerous programs. If you bring the kids along on a Friday, make sure you find out when story times are. Called Nature Tales for Tots, kids, especially preschoolers, can enjoy 40-minute programs, which include storytelling, puppet shows, and face painting. There is a $6 fee per child.

For area residents, the Stevens Nature Center offers a full slate of activities for children and adults. Special classes for kids, designed for accompaniment by a parent, highlight bats, owls, and other woodsy creatures. Call the center at (919) 387-5980 for more information.

Holden's Mill Trail

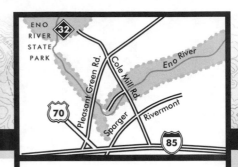

ENO RIVER STATE PARK

32

Pleasant Green Rd.

Cole Mill Rd.

Eno River

70

Sparger

Rivermont

85

IN BRIEF

Featuring the splash of the Eno River and the shade of tall trees, this is one of my favorite hikes in the area. After paralleling the Eno River—watch for herons!—you come to remnants of Holden's Mill, a gristmill built in 1811.

DIRECTIONS

From Durham, travel west on Interstate 85. Exit onto US 70 West. Almost immediately, turn right onto Pleasant Green Road. Turn left onto Cole Mill Road; follow it until it ends in Eno River State Park. Park at the first parking area (on the right, unmarked).

DESCRIPTION

A finer hike cannot be had in the Triangle area. Be sure to take your camera for this one. Like Park Ranger Lori Marlow, you might spot a rare yellow-crowned night heron feeding on crayfish from the river. Watch for other birds, including woodpeckers and indigo buntings.

To begin the hike, follow the signs that say River Access Trails. Take the lower leg of Buckquarter Creek Trail, which peels off to the right at Few's Ford. Follow the trail along the riverside and up, around, and over seriously large boulders. If you hike after heavy rains, footing is likely to be tricky. After the initial boulder scramble, you'll see evidence of beavers. Soon you'll find the footbridge that connects the Buckquarter Creek Trail to Holden's

KEY AT-A-GLANCE INFORMATION

Length:
4.1 miles

Configuration:
Figure 8

Difficulty:
Moderate

Scenery:
River views, remnants of 1820s gristmill, heron in the river

Exposure:
Shady

Solitude:
Moderately busy

Trail surface:
Dirt

Hiking time:
2.25 hours

Access:
No fees or permits

Maps:
Eno River State Park, Few's Ford Section

Facilities:
Rest rooms and water are at the park office

Special comments:
To reach the Holden's Mill Trail, you must first hike along the Buckquarter Creek Trail (see page 51).

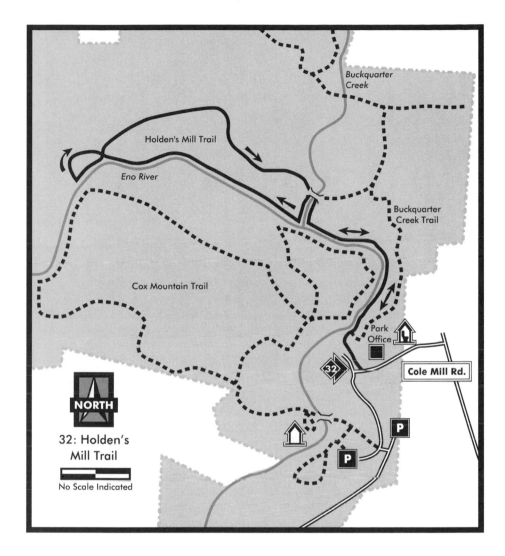

NORTH

32: Holden's Mill Trail

No Scale Indicated

Buckquarter Creek

Holden's Mill Trail

Eno River

Buckquarter Creek Trail

Cox Mountain Trail

Park Office

Cole Mill Rd.

Mill Trail. Cross over and follow the river. Be sure to notice the exposed, gnarled tree roots grasping onto the riverbanks. They're quite artistic in a natural way. Notice too, the lichen-covered trees and the grassy areas.

As you hike along the river, you'll have an occasional boulder scramble to negotiate, and just when you think you've lost the trail, you'll see that you simply go up and over the boulders to the right. The huge boulders make perfect studies for still-life photos. Plus, they do more than

that: They're evidently useful to the herons that search for freshwater mussels in the Eno. As you step down the trail, you're very likely to see shells left from herons who have dined al fresco.

Eventually you'll reach the Holden Mill Loop, at the very top of the trail, and the very best part of the hike. Turn left and continue around, keeping an eye out for the remains of Holden's Mill: sluice channels, stacked rock walls, and the old roadbeds leading to the gristmill. Be sure to look closely around the area:

Remnants of Holden's Mill in Eno River State Park.

The workforce of the mill was once large enough to support a school. When Thomas Holden sold the mill, he advertised it as having a six-room house with three fireplaces, a threshing machine, a saw mill, a cotton gin, an oil mill, and a corn and flour mill.

You'll return to the intersection and turn left. The last half of the hike crests a ridge before descending to the intersection with Buckquarter Creek Loop. Buckquarter Creek will add a moderate 1.5 miles to your hike but will also add some more great views of the Eno River. Near the top of the loop, look for some gnawed tree stumps fashioned by local beavers.

Inspiration Trail with Beech Trail Out-and-Back

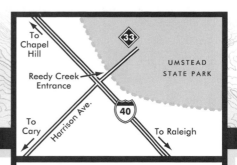

IN BRIEF

Want to take the kids out on a hike that's not too hard, but looks like a "real" mountain trail? If so, this is the hike you're looking for. It has enough hills and creeks to make it interesting, and it is loaded, curiously so, with more double- and triple-trunk trees than I've ever seen anywhere else.

DIRECTIONS

From Raleigh: Take the Wade Avenue Extension (west) and follow Umstead State Park signs to the Reedy Creek section of the park.

From Durham/Chapel Hill: Exit from Interstate 40 onto Harrison Avenue. Turn left and cross over Wade Avenue Extension following Umstead State Park signs to the Reedy Creek section of the park. The Inspiration Trail begins on the left at the bottom of the parking lot.

DESCRIPTION

Short and sweet, benches to sit on and admire the hardwoods dot this spiraling trail. From the Reedy Creek parking lot in Umstead Park, look for a gravel path that leads through the pine trees to the picnic shelter. You'll see the blue diamond-blazed Inspiration Trail split to the left, behind the picnic shelter

The trail first descends a hill to a creek; across the footbridge, the trail splits. Hike to the right up the hill, and you'll soon come to the Beech Trail,

KEY AT-A-GLANCE INFORMATION

Length:
2 miles

Configuration:
Balloon with spur

Difficulty:
Easy

Scenery:
Hardwood forest

Exposure:
Shady

Solitude:
Busy

Trail surface:
Roots, pine needles, rocks

Hiking time:
45 minutes

Access:
No fees or permits

Maps:
Umstead State Park

Facilities:
Rest rooms, water, picnic tables

Special comments:
Inspiration Trail is 1 mile; the Beech Trail out-and-back adds another mile.

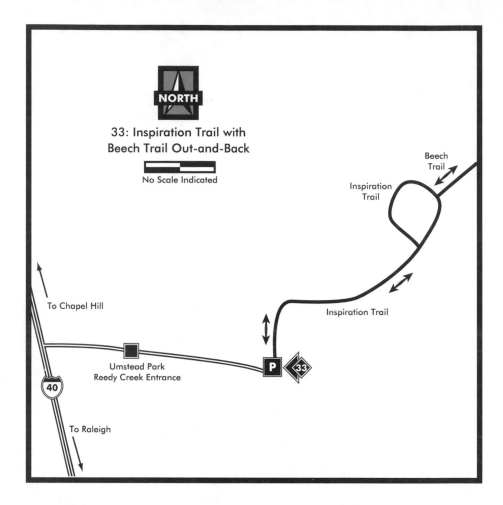

33: Inspiration Trail with
Beech Trail Out-and-Back

No Scale Indicated

Beech Trail

Inspiration Trail

To Chapel Hill

Inspiration Trail

Umstead Park
Reedy Creek Entrance

P 33

40

To Raleigh

which is marked with blue circles. You can add a mile to your total by turning right and hiking the Beech Trail as an out-and-back spur. The Beech Trail is primarily a connector between the Inspiration Trail and the Company Mill Loop. If you decide to press on and trek the Company Mill as well, you'll add 4.5 miles to your hike. Highlights of the Company Mill Loop include remains of an old mill washed away in 1929 and peaceful encounters with Crabtree and Sycamore Creeks.

After returning to Inspiration Trail, continue hiking counterclockwise. As you do, keep your eyes open for a series

of double- and triple-trunk trees. It's quite unusual to see so many so close together. The double-trunk pine tree in front of the triple-trunk elm tree has to be a highly unusual occurrence.

On the lower side of the Inspiration Trail you can see large mountain laurel blooming in the spring. When you complete the loop, turn right to return to the trailhead.

NEARBY ACTIVITIES

Just across I-40 from Umstead State Park is Lake Crabtree, another recreation area for hikers, boaters, and bikers. From the Reedy Creek entrance at Umstead, return to Interstate 40 and head northwest toward Chapel Hill. The exit onto Aviation Parkway for Crabtree Lake is approximately three miles. Just follow the signs. For information on canoe rentals, call ahead at (919) 460-3390. You won't have to worry about being swamped by speedboats here; gasoline-powered engines are not allowed on the lake. The kids and the family dog might enjoy the open play area. It's also a great space to throw a Frisbee or toss a football. The park is open daily from 8 a.m. to sunset. Call the number above for seasonal hours.

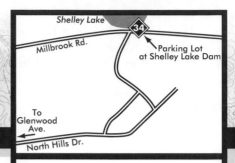

Shelley Lake

Millbrook Rd.

34

Parking Lot
at Shelley Lake Dam

To
Glenwood
Ave.

North Hills Dr.

Ironwood Ramble

IN BRIEF

Looking for a leisurely urban hike? This is it. This tree-lined hike winds through north-central Raleigh, away from popular Shelley Lake. The trees that line the path will make you feel as if you're farther away from heavy development than you are.

DIRECTIONS

In Raleigh: Go to Shelley Lake, which is located on Millbrook Road, between North Hills Drive and Lead Mine Road. Park in the lot below the dam and walk underneath Millbrook Road to start the hike.

DESCRIPTION

This area of forest is full of hardwoods, including the ironwood tree—the namesake of this greenway. Ironwood is a general name for trees with wood that is exceptionally hard. Examples of ironwood trees are members of the birch and beech families. Both are small deciduous trees. The birch ironwood has a slender trunk covered with flaking gray bark. Two of the beech ironwoods, the blue and water beech, have a blue-gray bark on their slender trunks.

The trail crosses three times over Lead Mine Creek, which it follows. After passing underneath both Millbrook and Shelley Lake Roads on a small decline, this greenway trail curves its way behind private homes. At 0.9 mile, the trail splits

KEY AT-A-GLANCE INFORMATION

Length:
2.5 miles

Configuration:
Balloon

Difficulty:
Easy

Scenery:
Homes, creeks

Exposure:
Shady

Solitude:
Busy

Trail surface:
Asphalt

Hiking time:
45 minutes

Access:
No fees or permits

Maps:
Capital Area Greenway Trail System or Raleigh Bike Map

Facilities:
Rest rooms and water at Shelley Lake

Special comments:
Hiking the Ironwood Greenway out-and-back contributes 1.6 miles to the hike. The North Hills Drive/ Ironwood Extension Loop adds another 0.9 mile.

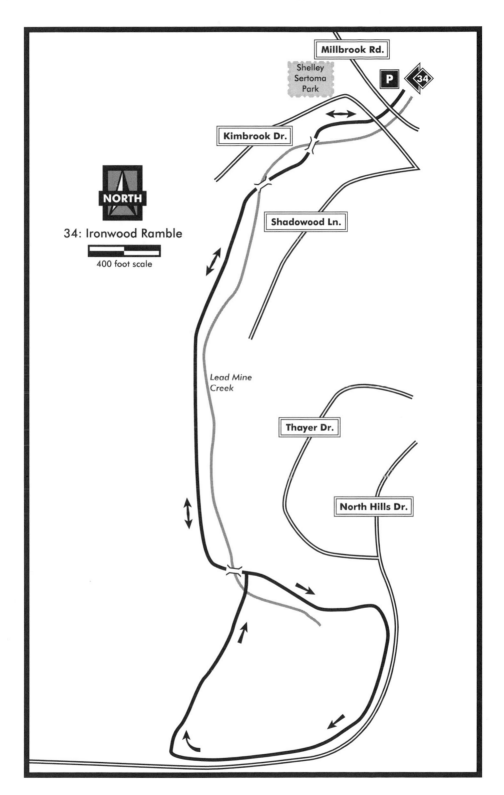

Millbrook Rd.

Shelley
Sertoma
Park

P 34

Kimbrook Dr.

Shadowood Ln.

NORTH

34: Ironwood Ramble

400 foot scale

*Lead Mine
Creek*

Thayer Dr.

North Hills Dr.

into two: To the left is the original Ironwood Trail, which ends on North Hills Drive; to the right and over the bridge is the Ironwood Trail Extension, a newer section.

Because the Ironwood Trail Extension also ends at North Hills Drive, 0.4 mile below where the original greenway ends, you make a balloon hike by using the sidewalk on North Hills Drive. Simply follow the original greenway trail to North Hills Drive. When you reach North Hills Drive, turn right and walk about 0.4 mile. Then turn right again back onto the newer asphalt of the Ironwood Trail Extension, which adds half a mile as it returns you to the original Ironwood Greenway Trail. Like most greenways, the Ironwood Trail is wheelchair traversible.

Once you return to the trailhead, you can choose to extend this hike; an obvious choice would be to continue around the Shelley Lake Trail. This paved three-mile trail circles the lake, returning you to the parking area where you began the Ironwood Ramble. After passing beneath Millbrook Road, continue past your car and over a bridge. At the intersection of Shelley Lake Trail, turn left and walk

toward the Sertoma Arts Center. The trail then descends into a section of birch trees. Take advantage of the exercise stations through here to exercise more than your legs. Above the lake the trail intersects the lake loop trail. At the upper end of the lake, a boardwalk and side loop trail extend over a marshy area. The trail begins to head west and then south back to the Sertoma Arts Center.

A note of discretion for the wary hiker: Due caution should always be exercised when hiking in an urban environment. Although as relatively safe as any greenway in Raleigh, in the past there have been postings around the Shelley Lake Greenway warning trail users of attacks. Although the incidents were considered isolated, it always pays to be cautious.

NEARBY ACTIVITIES

Located at 1400 West Millbrook Road, the Sertoma Arts Center is near the entrance to Shelley Lake. Although primarily a hands-on arts facility for Raleigh residents, interested visitors are welcome. Look for special events at the center such as concerts and art openings. The center's phone number is (919) 420-2329.

Lake Benson Trail

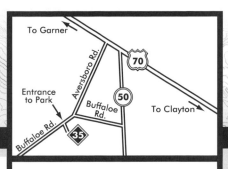

IN BRIEF

Easy! This hike circles the perimeter of Lake Benson Park in Garner and passes through a large grassy playing field. Depending on when you go, you may see lots of dogs and their owners playing Frisbee in the fields.

DIRECTIONS

Just south of Raleigh, Lake Benson is located in Garner on Buffaloe Road (off NC 50), three miles south of the intersection of US 70 East and NC 50 South. Turn left when Buffaloe Road hits Aversboro Road. The park is 0.2 mile to your left.

DESCRIPTION

Lake Benson, the water reservoir for Garner, has been turned into a city park. There's a lot of open space here, and there's no telling what you might see going on when you visit. On my first trip I was pleasantly surprised to see dogs and their owners having some sort of Frisbee contest. A favorite spot for community gatherings and family reunions, Lake Benson is also a very popular picnic area. Near the picnic shelters are playgrounds with swings and jungle gyms to keep the kids busy. The largest event each year is a town concert and fireworks show on July 3.

The trail loops the playing fields and the lake and has a number of benches on

KEY AT-A-GLANCE INFORMATION

Length:
1.3 miles

Configuration:
Loop

Difficulty:
Easy

Scenery:
Lake Benson, playing fields

Exposure:
Mostly sunny

Solitude:
Busy

Trail surface:
Fine gravel

Hiking time:
30 minutes

Access:
No fees or permits

Maps:
None

Facilities:
Rest rooms, water, picnic shelters, grills, basketball court

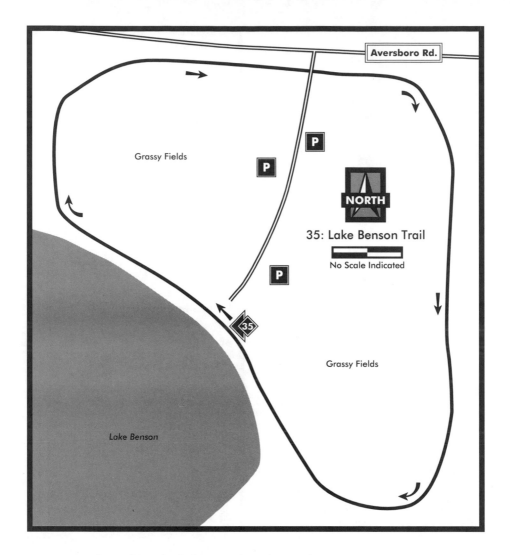

Aversboro Rd.

Grassy Fields

P

P

NORTH

35: Lake Benson Trail

No Scale Indicated

P

35

Grassy Fields

Lake Benson

it. To access the trail, just look for any of the spokes that hook into it, pick a direction, and start walking. As you walk along, be sure to note how sandy the soil is—a clear sign that Garner sits on the upper edge of the coastal plain. Another clear sign of the area's coastal nature are the tall pine trees.

A pleasant town, Garner traces its roots back to the 1850s. The development of railroads through the farmland stimulated population growth. By 1878, Garner had acquired a post office and

begun the process of incorporating as a town, which occurred in 1905. The town grew slowly from a farming community, graduating in the 1950s to bedroom community status for Raleigh. With the town becoming a satellite of Raleigh, transportation between the two was improved with the broadening and relocating of US 70. Garner remains a small town and a nice retreat for folks who work in Raleigh but who don't necessarily want to live there.

NEARBY ACTIVITIES

For a bite to eat, we've already mentioned A Place to Eat (see page 95). Here are a few others: Rudino's Pizza & Grinders/ Grandma Eva's Coffee & Bread Company, 2644 Timber Drive, (919) 661-8008; Applebee's Neighborhood Bar & Grill, 1165 US 70 West, (919) 661-9505; Toot-N-Tell Family Restaurant (southern/barbecue), 903 Old Garner Road, (919) 772-2616.

Lake Crabtree Trail

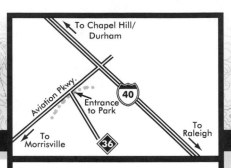

IN BRIEF

This wide trail circles panoramic Lake Crabtree in Lake Crabtree County Park. The first half of this trail qualifies this hike as one of the best in the Triangle, because it's wooded and shady as well as pleasantly hilly. The second half, however, is a bit difficult, because several areas that the trail traverses are truly swampy in all but the driest weather.

DIRECTIONS

Turn onto Aviation Parkway from Interstate 40 and drive toward Morrisville. Lake Crabtree County Park will be shortly on the left. To access the trail, park in the lot near the boat ramp and walk up the park road as if you're exiting the park. The crosswalk signals that the trail is near.

DESCRIPTION

There's no two ways about it: The Lake Trail, around the edges of 520-acre Lake Crabtree, is the trickiest path to hike in the Triangle. Parts of the Lake Trail coincide with the Highland Loop Trail, which is very popular with mountain bikers but closed during wet weather to protect it. During those times, the Lake Trail will be closed as well.

At first, this trail can't be beaten: The path is wide, the views of the lake superb, the poison ivy beaten back from trail's edge. Just after you cross the first wooden bridge, you'll bear to the right.

KEY AT-A-GLANCE INFORMATION

Length:
5.2 miles
Configuration:
Loop, if you do the whole thing
Difficulty:
Easy until you hit the swamp.
Scenery:
Lake views, reptiles of all sorts, cat tails, highways
Exposure:
Part shade/part sun
Solitude:
Could be by yourself on back half
Trail surface:
Dirt, pine needle, asphalt, grass, mud
Hiking time:
2 hours
Access:
No fees or permits
Maps:
Available at the station as you turn into the park.
Facilities:
Rest rooms, water, horseshoes, volleyball, picnic shelters; sailboats, canoes and rowboats for rent
Special comments:
Lake Crabtree is also home to the Highland Loop Trail, a mountain bike trail built and maintained in part by NC FATS. As much as you might want to hike this trail, please don't.

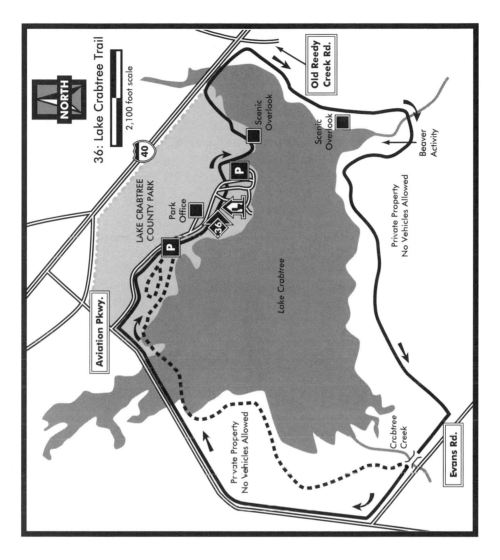

36: Lake Crabtree Trail

NORTH

2,100 foot scale

40

LAKE CRABTREE COUNTY PARK

Park Office

36

P

P

P

Scenic Overlook

Scenic Overlook

Old Reedy Creek Rd.

Beaver Activity

Private Property No Vehicles Allowed

Lake Crabtree

Aviation Pkwy.

Private Property No Vehicles Allowed

Crabtree Creek

Evans Rd.

(The red trail is a connector to the Highland Trail.) As you continue, you'll arrive at the Heather Carr Memorial Overlook. Be sure to walk up on the deck and take a look at the lake.

Continuing, you'll begin to hear the noise of Interstate 40 and see a connector path that links the gravel roads in Umstead Park that are used by mountain bikers with the Highland Loop. What you should do, however, is to continue walking alongside the lake, up the hill, and through the metal gate.

At the gate, the Lake Trail and the Black Creek Greenway in Cary run together until the two paths split just before the Weston Parkway overpass. Walk to the right to follow the blue-blazed Lake Trail behind several office buildings. You'll see the occasional footpath leading from the buildings to the trail. Soon, however, you'll see a sign indicating that the trail is wet. Unless you like swamp hiking, this is the time to turn back.

If you continue, you'll come to an enormous patch of poison ivy. After you tiptoe and high-step through that evil weed, you'll see cattails, yet another signal that the trail is worsening. If you forge ahead, you'll probably find yourself up to your ankles in mud. Plans are in the works, however, for boardwalks to span this area.

Look for a road up ahead and walk toward it. Walk to the right, alongside the road, until the trail becomes clear again on your right. If you want to step down to the trail to walk along the marvelous bridge over Crabtree Creek, do, but be sure to return to the road because the trail becomes completely obliterated just past the turn into the woods.

Stick to the road, and respect the No Trespassing sign posted at one of the offices that back up to Lake Crabtree. Just walk to the right through the parking lots until you see a stop light up and to your left on Aviation Parkway. From here on in, you're road-walking back to the park, about 0.3 to 0.4 mile away. Walk down to the very last parking lot where you left your car, and call it a day.

Lake Johnson Trail

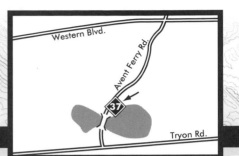

IN BRIEF

This enormously popular trail, part of the Raleigh Greenway system, circles Lake Johnson. Take along stale bread and crackers to feed the waterfowl population that is slowly but surely making Lake Johnson home.

DIRECTIONS

From Raleigh on Interstate 440 heading south, exit left onto Athens Drive. Head west, and then turn onto Avent Ferry Road. Travel until the Lake Johnson boathouse comes into view on the left. You can park here in the lot or travel across the causeway and park in the lot to the left. If the trail is crowded, some parking can be had along Avent Ferry Road.

DESCRIPTION

Built in 1955 by the Army Corps of Engineers as a drinking water reservoir for the city of Raleigh, Lake Johnson hosts one of the most popular hikes in the area. Because of the way the trail is designed, you can hike anywhere from 3.5 to 5.5 miles without passing the same territory twice.

My favorite way to hike this trail is to park in the lot in front of the newly renovated visitor center and boathouse and head left into the woods away from the wooden bridge. From this direction, the trail appears to be a flat, winding path—perfect for warming up your leg muscles. Along the way you'll see the

KEY AT-A-GLANCE INFORMATION

Length:
5.5 miles

Configuration:
Figure 8

Difficulty:
Moderate

Scenery:
People watching, coots waiting to be fed

Exposure:
Shady

Solitude:
Very busy

Trail surface:
Asphalt on the boathouse side; part asphalt, part dirt on the other side

Hiking time:
1.6 hours

Access:
No fees or permits

Maps:
Capital Area Greenway Trail System Map or Raleigh Bike Map

Facilities:
Rest rooms, concessions, pedal boats, educational programs

Special comments:
Be careful when crossing Avent Ferry Road; it's very busy.

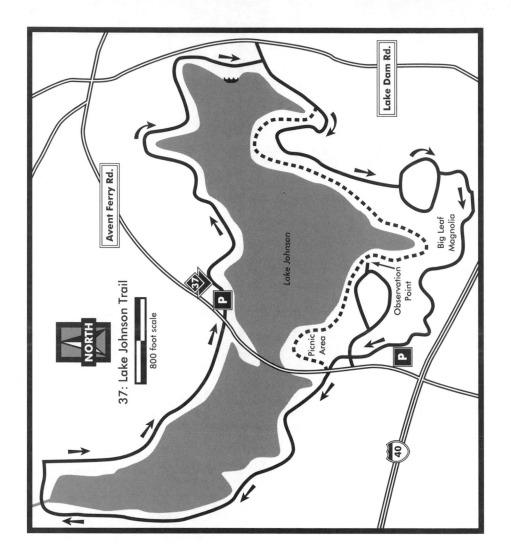

occasional bench and picnic table, and you'll be sure to pass lots of dog walkers and mountain bike riders, in addition to the usual complement of runners. When you reach the dam, you're likely to see dog owners pitching sticks into the lake for their would-be retrievers to retrieve.

After you cross the dam, however, the trail changes its personality and becomes quite hilly—so hilly, in fact—that you might start wishing for one of those benches to appear. You'll also see several branching paths that allow you to walk close to the water or up on the bluffs above the lake.

Regardless of whether you meander close to the water or not, you'll eventually come to a decision point: Do you cross Avent Ferry Road and continue hiking the rougher portion of the trail, or do you continue to your right and cross the wooden bridge? If you continue to the right, down to the wooden bridge, you can wrap up a pleasant 3.5-mile hike by watching a plethora of waterfowl paddling near the bridge.

Occasionally the noise from Interstate 40 is loud, but the fun of watching the ducks, mallards, coots, gulls, and geese makes up for the auditory disturbance.

If, however, you cross Avent Ferry Road, you can add another 2 miles to the 3.5 you've already logged. This "backside" of the lake is substantially rougher than the paved path, but it's just as appealing. The trail winds westward, leading to a retaining wall that overlooks a small waterfall. Later you'll pass a spur trail that leads to Lake Johnson Pool.

When you reach the flat, bark-chip-surfaced portion of the trail, you'll know you're nearing the end, and soon enough you'll arrive at Avent Ferry Road, in front of the boathouse. Be careful crossing that road!

Even when you finish your walk, you may find yourself wanting to linger at Lake Johnson. The newly remodeled boathouse features the area's best deck and lake overlook.

NEARBY ACTIVITIES

For lunch or dinner after an hour—or a day—at Lake Johnson, a robust meal might be in order. There are several restaurants to choose from near the park. Continue on Avent Ferry Road, which will take you across Lake Johnson. Turn right on I-40 and watch for the Crossroads Boulevard exit. This exit will carry you into the Crossroads Plaza, where you'll find several restaurants.

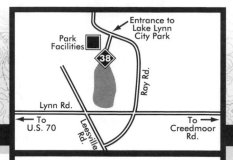

Lake Lynn Greenway

IN BRIEF

This Raleigh Greenway trail, located off Ray Road, loops Lake Lynn, which must surely be the Venice Beach of Raleigh. Because the path has both pavement and boardwalks, you'll very likely see people on rollerblades and bicycles in addition to the regular joggers and walkers.

DIRECTIONS

Lake Lynn can be accessed in two ways. The first is by Lynn Road, east of Glenwood Avenue. Look for a gravel parking lot. The other is via the main entrance at 7921 Ray Road.

DESCRIPTION

Part of the citywide Capital Area Greenways developed in 1976, Lynn Park symbolizes Raleigh's desire to mingle urban development with a practical plan for preservation and use of the city's natural beauty. A greenway and more, Lake Lynn is a full-service recreation area. The park has lighted ballfields, tennis courts, and a modern facility to host everything from baby showers to weddings (or vice versa). It has been described as having that "planned community" feel, which some folks abhor and others adore. An online guide to the Triangle area describes the greenway's paved surface as "baby-bottom smooth."

Throughout the year, you'll find lots of interesting programs to take, too. Among the classes you might find

KEY AT-A-GLANCE INFORMATION

Length:
2.2 miles

Configuration:
Balloon

Difficulty:
Easy

Scenery:
Lake; waterfowl, especially geese

Exposure:
Part shade/part sun

Solitude:
None

Trail surface:
Paved and boardwalk

Hiking time:
45 minutes

Access:
No fees or permits

Maps:
Capital Area Greenway Trail System or Raleigh Bike Map

Facilities:
Rest rooms, water, and picnic tables are found in or near the community center building near Ray Road.

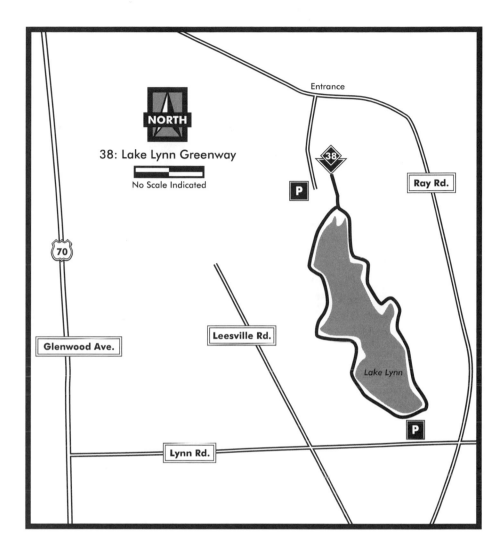

NORTH

38: Lake Lynn Greenway

No Scale Indicated

Entrance

38

Ray Rd.

P

70

Glenwood Ave.

Leesville Rd.

Lake Lynn

P

Lynn Rd.

offered at Lake Lynn are step aerobics, weight training, calligraphy, street hock-ey, needle arts, and yoga.

Several apartment complexes surround Lake Lynn, so the trail is typically quite crowded, even on cold days. But the geese and mallards who have started mak-ing the lake home don't seem to mind.

Though this is a lakeside hike, don't expect it to be flat. There are several rolling hills that will get your attention. Come early or late to this popular park and you should have the company of runners, hikers, and even a few mellow

practitioners of Eastern meditation and exercise.

NEARBY ACTIVITIES
After your urban oneness with Lake Lynn, why not head south to the Atlanta Bread Company & Cafe, 7400-2 Six Forks Road, (919) 845-0030. To get there, exit Lake Lynn Park and turn left onto Lynn Road. Follow Lynn Road until you reach Six Forks Road. Turn left onto Six Forks, drive and watch on your right for the Peachtree Shopping Center where the restaurant is located.

Walkers enjoying the Lake Lynn Greenway.

Little Creek Trail

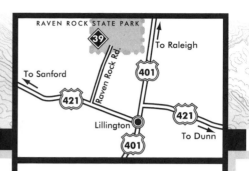

IN BRIEF

This kid-friendly hike contains something of a cliché: a babbling brook. Along the trail, look for an exceptionally tall, old cedar and listen for the noise that sounds just like someone laughing.

DIRECTIONS

From Raleigh: Travel south on US 401 to Lillington. At the intersection of US 421 and US 401 in downtown Lillington, turn right onto US 421. Follow the signs to Raven Rock State Park. Trails begin from the left, center, and right of the parking lot. Little Creek Trail is accessed from Raven Rock Loop Trail, which departs from the right side of the parking area.

DESCRIPTION

Located in the Cape Fear River Basin, Little Creek exposes the underlying bedrock of the area as it undulates through the woods to the Cape Fear River. River birch, beech, and sycamore trees tower above the riverbanks. In places, you'll see miniature gorges and waterfalls. This is a great hike for kids. The trail is short but has plenty of gnarled roots and rocks in the path. Tennis shoes might do for those with strong ankles, but a pair of light hiking boots are recommended.

To access the Little Creek Loop, you must first hike along the popular Raven Rock Loop Trail. (The round-trip on

KEY AT-A-GLANCE INFORMATION

Length:
1.4 miles

Configuration:
Balloon

Difficulty:
Easy

Scenery:
River banks, waterfalls

Exposure:
Shady

Solitude:
Busy on weekends

Trail surface:
Dirt, leaves, sandy near the creek

Hiking time:
30 minutes

Access:
No fees or permits

Maps:
Raven Rock State Park

Facilities:
Rest rooms, water, picnic tables, snack machines

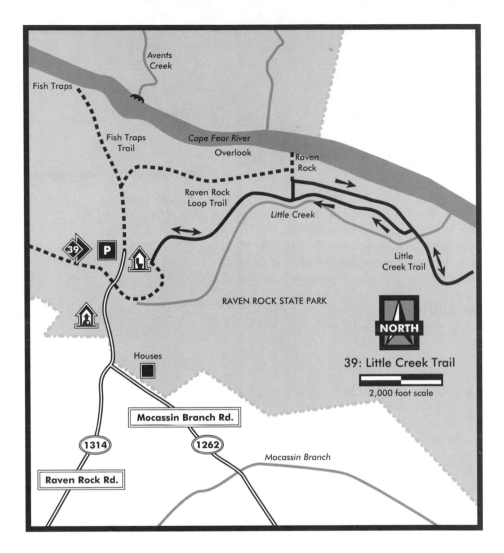

Raven Rock Loop is 2 miles long.) Soon, however, you'll see the Little Creek Trail split off from the Raven Rock Loop.

NEARBY ACTIVITIES

At the end of the hike, you can check out the canoe put-in and the group camping facilities. The wilderness family campground and the canoe campground have tent pads, fire circles, and pit toilets. Call the park at (910) 893-4888 for more information. If you're interested in

paddling, the Harnett County Historical Society (P.O. Box 1865, Lillington, NC 27546) publishes a brochure explaining opportunities for camping your way down the Cape Fear River Trail.

The nearest town to Raven Rock is Lillington, 6 miles to the east. Located in Harnett County, 28 miles south of Raleigh, Lillington was settled in the early 1700s by Highland Scots who staked their claim in the area near the Cape Fear River. British settlers, old enemies of the Scots, also settled in this area. During the Revolutionary War, Scots settlers were forced to promise not to take up arms against British settlers fighting against King George. A site near Lillington is reported to have been the scene of a mass execution of supposed Scots "traitors."

The town has several fast-food restaurants. Located primarily along Main Street, the choices are not gourmet but should whet your body's craving for carbohydrates (and maybe a little fat too): Hardee's, Dairy Queen, Howard's Barbecue, and others.

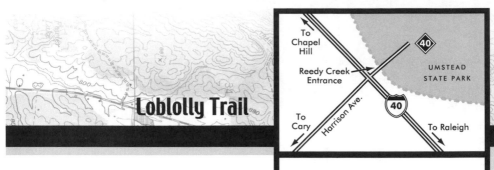

Loblolly Trail

IN BRIEF

This is another long-distance hike for you hiking monsters out there! Look for lots of variety along this footpath: the tall pines in Umstead State Park, the dam located in the Richland Greenway section, the research groves of Schenck Forest, and finally, the remnants of the original trail that meets the Wade Avenue Extension.

DIRECTIONS

From Raleigh: From the Wade Avenue Extension (west), follow Umstead State Park signs to the Reedy Creek section of the park.

From Durham/Chapel Hill: Exit from Interstate 40 onto Harrison Avenue. Turn left and cross over the Wade Avenue Extension, following Umstead State Park signs to the Reedy Creek section of the park. The Loblolly Trail begins at the bottom of the right side of the parking area.

DESCRIPTION

The Loblolly Trail is moderately difficult, not so much because of the terrain as because of its length. If you hike this trail, you'll discover that it has four distinct sections, three of which are enjoyable. Section four is for the muley-headed hikers like me.

The first three miles, all inside Umstead State Park, gently roll over ridges, passing through storm-damaged areas and providing pleasant views of Reedy Creek as it winds through the

KEY AT-A-GLANCE INFORMATION

Length:
10 miles round-trip

Configuration:
Out-and-back

Difficulty:
Difficult, due to distance and occasionally rough trail conditions

Scenery:
Excellent to poor, depending upon the section

Exposure:
Filtered sun

Solitude:
Moderate

Trail surface:
Dirt

Hiking time:
6 hours

Access:
No fees or permits

Maps:
Capital Area Greenway Trail System Map No. 17 shows the entire path; however, be aware that it still shows it as a 6-mile trail.

Facilities:
Rest rooms, water, picnic tables in Umstead Park

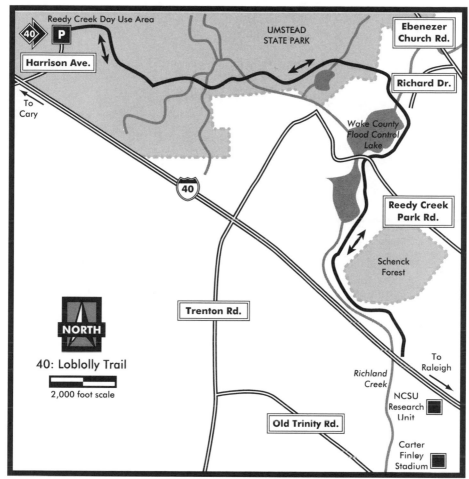

Reedy Creek Day Use Area

40

P

Harrison Ave.

To Cary

UMSTEAD STATE PARK

Ebenezer Church Rd.

Richard Dr.

Wake County Flood Control Lake

40

Reedy Creek Park Rd.

Schenck Forest

NORTH

40: Loblolly Trail

2,000 foot scale

Trenton Rd.

To Raleigh

Richland Creek

NCSU Research Unit

Old Trinity Rd.

Carter Finley Stadium

park. You'll also cross two gravel bike paths (at approximately two miles, and again just before the trail passes out of the park) that will allow you to be creative about your hiking route.

Throughout this section, you'll see many loblolly pines, a staple of North Carolina coastal forests. The Loblolly pine, an important tree to the North Carolina economy, is used for building material, barrel staves, pulpwood, and laths.

Mile four is a transition mile. It begins in the park but then crosses outside. Once outside the park, the Loblolly Trail is blazed white, like the Appalachian Trail. At first you pass through a flood plain, and then you have to scale an

earthen dam. (Be aware that the trail is not marked in this section.) But scale the dam wall, enjoy the view, and then look for a sign to the left of the dam marking the Richland Creek Greenway Trail. This section of the trail runs very close to the backyards of private homes.

Before the fourth mile is over, you cross Reedy Creek Road, a gravel road that actually intersects Umstead State Park about three-quarters of a mile to the right. Cross the road and look for the white blazes near the bridge down to your right. Once you leave the road, you will cross into the lower side of Schenck Forest, a forest used by NC State forestry students.

Dogs enjoying a swim in Reedy Creek.

Schenck Forest, the third section, contains about 1.5 miles of the trail, bringing the total distance to 5 miles. As you walk through the forest, you'll see various memorials to NCSU forestry professors as well as explanatory and interpretive signs. Heed any instructions you may see posted in this section of the forest, since it does serve educational purposes.

Near the end of the Schenck Forest section the trail becomes difficult to follow due to storm damage and timber harvesting. However, try to follow Richland Creek and keep the road noise from the Wade Avenue Extension to your right. You'll know you've left Schenck Forest when you see the cement cones denoting a water easement.

This fourth section of the trail (mile six) is the oldest and most confusing section. The trail once led to Carter-Finley stadium; however, due to construction, most of the trail past the square culvert has been obliterated. This section of the trail is quite mushy, and noisy due to the traffic. It's also likely that the area will be flooded. Unless reaching the culvert represents a personal badge of hiking-distance honor, end the hike at the border of Schenck Forest and return the way you came.

Neuse River Trail

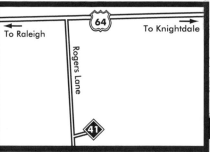

To Raleigh — 64 — To Knightdale

Rogers Lane

41

IN BRIEF

This trail provides excellent views of the Neuse River. If you're looking for a nice long path to break in some boots or watch for herons, this trail is the perfect choice. Though it follows the river for the most part, the trail is far from level. In fact, you'll discover several good hills.

DIRECTIONS

Drive east out of Raleigh on US 64. Rogers Lane appears about two miles out of town. (If you cross the Neuse River Bridge, you've gone too far.) Turn right onto it. Proceed down Rogers Lane until it dead-ends and you see a new parking lot to the left. Look for and follow a dirt trail down a small hill. When you reach the river, do not go toward the railroad tracks; go instead to the left, as if you're walking toward the houses. After about a quarter mile, you'll see a Raleigh Greenway sign to the left, and the grassy path becomes obvious.

DESCRIPTION

Once you're on the path, just put your feet in go gear and your mind in cruise mode. Enjoy the river as you walk along viewing the swamp and environment of an upland forest greenway.

About halfway in, you'll come to a paved road. Turn right, walk 0.1 mile, and then climb a steep hill up to the left. Other than that, this is an easy trail to follow. When you've had half of the dis-

KEY AT-A-GLANCE INFORMATION

Length:
8 miles

Configuration:
Out-and-back

Difficulty:
Moderate, due to distance

Scenery:
Neuse River

Exposure:
Mostly sunny

Solitude:
Minimally busy

Trail surface:
Mostly grass, some pavement, some dirt path

Hiking time:
2.5 hours

Access:
No fees or permits

Maps:
This relatively new greenway path should be on the next edition of the Capital Area Greenway Trail System Map

Facilities:
None

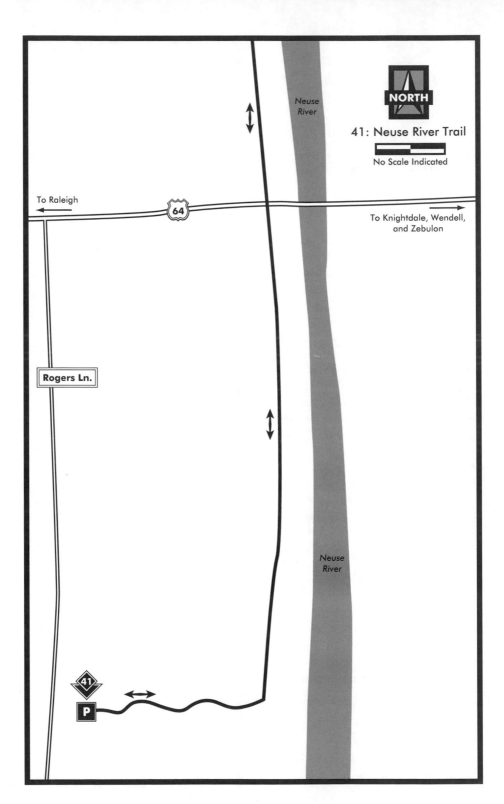

NORTH

41: Neuse River Trail

No Scale Indicated

Neuse River

To Raleigh

64

To Knightdale, Wendell, and Zebulon

Rogers Ln.

Neuse River

41

P

tance you want, turn around and retrace your steps.

As you walk along the Neuse River, consider both its history and its future. The Neuse gained its English name in 1584 from Arthur Barlow, an explorer who had come to North Carolina at the request of Sir Walter Raleigh. Barlow named it for the Neusiok Indians he found living near the river along the coast. (The Native Americans had a different name for the river, calling it GOW-TO-NO, their phrase for "pine in the river".)

Later the Neuse became important to the development of Raleigh. One of the earlier economic forces in the area was Raleigh's function as a break bulk station, where freight was changed over from ship to wagon on its westward trek. This transformation happened in Raleigh because of the Fall Line, where the coastal plain meets the rolling hills of the Piedmont, and where rivers become much more difficult to navigate.

The Neuse River is one of seven rivers that drain the eastern banks of the Blue Ridge mountains. An estimated 14% of North Carolina's population lives inside the Neuse watershed, which is why in recent years efforts have been steadily increasing to protect the Neuse.

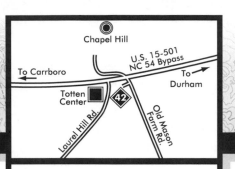

Chapel Hill

To Carrboro

U.S. 15-501
NC 54 Bypass

To Durham

Totten Center

42

Laurel Hill Rd.

Old Mason Farm Rd.

North Carolina Botanical Garden Ramble

IN BRIEF

If you like mountainous terrain, put this hike on your list. It traverses an area that is similar to the mountains of western North Carolina. In April you can see dwarf irises and wild azaleas blooming along the trails.

DIRECTIONS

From Raleigh, travel into Chapel Hill on US 54 West, and exit onto the 15/501 Bypass just south of town. From Durham, travel into Chapel Hill via 15/501, taking the bypass around town. The North Carolina Botanical Garden is located just off the 15/501 Bypass on the south side of Chapel Hill. Look for brown signs pointing to the entrance, which is on Old Mason Farm Road. Once you make the turn, look for a smallish sign adjacent to the gravel road that marks the entrance to the parking area.

DESCRIPTION

The North Carolina Botanical Garden is supported by the State of North Carolina and by the Botanical Garden Foundation, Inc. If you've never been, then make time to go. Not only can you enjoy a nice woodland walk, you can visit the formal gardens to see what's blooming.

From the gravel parking lot, walk down a path to the information station. (Here you'll see signs pointing to the Totten Center, to the right. Save a stroll through these cultivated gardens for last.)

KEY AT-A-GLANCE INFORMATION

Length:
1.5 miles

Configuration:
A very lumpy figure 8

Difficulty:
Moderate

Scenery:
Woodlands

Exposure:
Shady

Solitude:
Road noise reminds you that you're not in a remote area; plus, the area is popular with Chapel Hill residents.

Trail surface:
Dirt

Hiking time:
45 minutes

Access:
No fees or permits; the nature trails are open dawn to dusk.

Maps:
Available at the information station at the trailhead

Facilities:
Rest rooms and water at the Totten Center

Special comments:
The red–blazed Oak Hickory Trail is 1.1 miles long; the yellow–blazed Streamside Trail adds 0.3 mile.

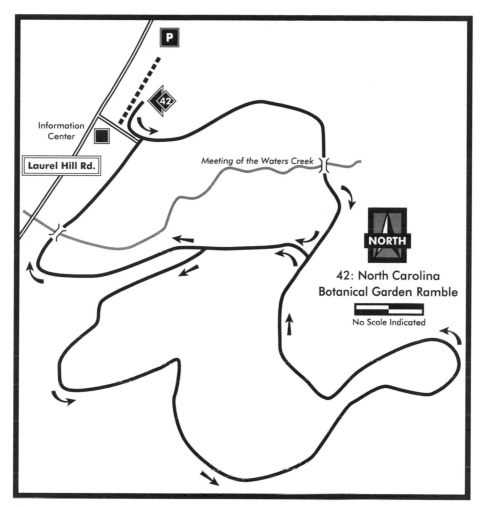

42

Information
Center

Laurel Hill Rd.

Meeting of the Waters Creek

NORTH

42: North Carolina
Botanical Garden Ramble

No Scale Indicated

The Botanical Garden provides interpretive sheets.

Turn left at the information station and follow the yellow-numbered posts to the left. Just past Post 9, the trail crosses Meeting of the Waters Creek, which once provided water to the University of North Carolina many, many years ago.

After crossing the creek, you'll ascend a hill. Here you'll see a post with red markings indicating the beginning of the Oak-Hickory Trail. Don't take it; stay with the yellow-marked streamside trail.

Just past Post 12, you'll see a red-marked post indicating another opportunity to walk on the Oak-Hickory Trail.

This time, take the spur and begin walking uphill. Posts through here are lettered (beginning with F) and will descend. When you reach the letter B, be sure to take the out-and-back spur to the right before continuing straight on to letter A.

At Post A, continue right, down the hill. Soon you'll come to the yellow Post 11. Turn left, and once again walk to Post 12. This time, however, continue walking to Posts 13–17. Just beyond Post 17 is the information station where you started.

Once you reach the information station, walk across the paved road to the Totten Center to stroll through the cultivated gardens. Sections contain coastal

Paul Green Cabin located in the North Carolina Botanical Garden.

plants, mountain habitat plants, aquatic plants, poisonous and carnivorous plants, as well as a national collection of rosemary plants.

The Totten Center is open weekdays throughout the year from 8 a.m. to 5 p.m. Weekend hours are 10 a.m. to 5 p.m. on Saturdays, 1 to 5 p.m. on Sundays. During Daylight Savings time, weekend hours are 9 a.m. to 6 p.m. on Saturdays and 1 to 6 p.m. on Sundays.

Although you never completely escape road noise, as my good friend Ellen said, you can enjoy a short, woodsy hike here.

NEARBY ACTIVITIES

Unless you can't spare the time, visit the main garden just across the road from the trail. There you can find native southeastern plants arranged according to their preferred habitat—coastal plain, sandhill, mountain, and an extensive herb garden. Be sure to visit the nationally recognized collection of rosemary shrubs—there are over 400 varieties!—and look for the collection of poisonous plants. From April until October, the Botanical Garden sells wildflowers and herbs, so if you're interested, you can take a reminder of your hike home and plant it in your yard.

Northington Ferry

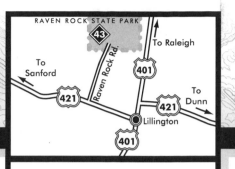

RAVEN ROCK STATE PARK
43
To Raleigh
To Sanford
401
To Dunn
421
Raven Rock Rd.
421
401
Lillington

IN BRIEF

This hike travels through pine forests down to the mouth of Campbell Creek. Here, in the late 1700s, Jesse Northington built and operated a ferry, which crossed the Cape Fear River between Fayetteville and Raleigh.

DIRECTIONS

From Raleigh: Travel south on US 401 to Lillington. At the intersection of US 421 and US 401 in downtown Lillington, turn right onto US 421. Follow the signs to Raven Rock State Park. Trails begin from the left, center, and right of the parking lot. Northington Ferry Trail begins at the center trailhead.

DESCRIPTION

This trail is an easy walk through a mostly pine forest, down to the Cape Fear River to a spot where Jesse Northington operated a ferry. (To give you some idea of the time line, Jesse Northington died in 1827.) Samuel Northington, Jesse's father, came to the area from Leers, England. He was among the first settlers in the area.

As you walk through the pines, consider that this region of North Carolina was once known for its production of naval stores, tar and turpentine products rendered from the pine trees. The pine trees would be slashed with diagonal cuts so that the sap could be easily collected. The cutting, of course, seriously

KEY AT-A-GLANCE INFORMATION

Length:
2.2 miles

Configuration:
Out-and-back

Difficulty:
Easy, except for the descent to the river

Scenery:
Great views of the Cape Fear River

Exposure:
Filtered sun

Solitude:
Very busy

Trail surface:
Sandy gravel

Hiking time:
1.2 hours

Access:
No fees or permits

Maps:
Raven Rock State Park

Facilities:
Rest rooms, water, picnic tables, snack machines

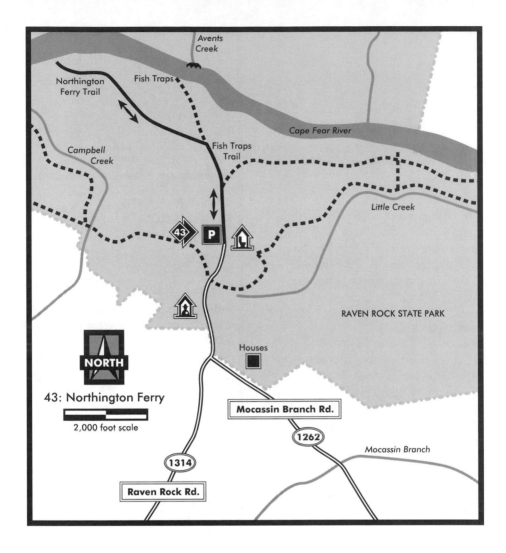

Avents
Creek

Northington
Ferry Trail

Fish Traps

Cape Fear River

Campbell
Creek

Fish Traps
Trail

Little Creek

43 **P**

RAVEN ROCK STATE PARK

NORTH

43: Northington Ferry

2,000 foot scale

Houses

Mocassin Branch Rd.

1262

1314

Mocassin Branch

Raven Rock Rd.

harmed the trees. Occasionally in muse-
ums found in this part of the state house
remnants of such "turpentine" trees.

(The Museum of the Cape Fear, located in Fayetteville, is home to one of the
trees. Though the museum is out of the
60-mile scope of this book, you can call
the museum at 910-486-1330 for more
information.)

If you have read *Cold Mountain* by
Charles Frazier, it won't take much to
wonder if Inman, the protagonist of the
novel, crossed the Cape Fear River near

a ferry station such as this one. It's lucky
for us that today the Cape Fear is a
cleaner river than it was when Inman
crossed it.

After parking your vehicle, locate the
middle trail at the trailhead. This will
lead you to three trails: Northington
Ferry, Fish Traps, and Raven Rock Loop.
Northington Ferry branches off to the
left and leads to the Cape Fear River.
The trail ends at the confluence of the
Cape Fear River and Campbell Creek.
(Incidentally, the English weren't the

136

only settlers in the area, as the name "Campbell" indicates. Many of the early settlers hailed from Scotland.)

It's an out-and-back, so head back the way you came in to relocate the trailhead, where there are rest rooms, a phone, and picnic tables. If you would like to extend your hike, but not by much, then veer back to your left when you reach the Fish Traps Trail, where you can seethe remains of the the ferry and dam locks. This trail also is an out-and-back and will add another mile to your hike.

The Fish Traps Trail will lead you back to the Cape Fear, but at a point farther south than the Northington Ferry Trail intersection with the river.

Occoneechee Mountain Trail/Brown Elfin Trail

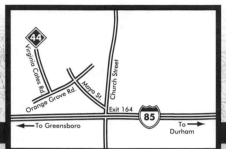

IN BRIEF

If you're starved for long-distance views, hiking these two trails will take the edge off your hunger. The vista of northern Orange County and the Eno River from the bluffs of Occoneechee Mountain, one of the highest points in Orange County at 867 feet, is excellent.

DIRECTIONS

From Durham, travel Interstate 85 to Exit 164. Turn north onto Churton Street. Turn left at the stoplight onto Mayo Street, about 50 yards from I-85. Turn left at the stop sign on Orange Grove Road. Turn right on Virginia Cates Road and follow the signs to the parking area.

DESCRIPTION

John Lederer, a German doctor and explorer, first passed through the area in 1670. He noted the presence of both the Occoneechee Indians, a tribe with roots in the Eastern Sioux, and the Great Trading Path, a trade route that ran down from Virginia and then west to the Catawba Indians. (Today, I-85 roughly follows part of the Great Trading Path.) By 1701, however, when John Lawson passed through the area, the Occoneechee Indians had vanished. No one knows what exactly happened to them.

While the fate of the Indians remains somewhat a mystery, the geologic significance of the area does not. Some

KEY AT-A-GLANCE INFORMATION

Length:
About 2 miles

Configuration:
Loop with cut-through

Difficulty:
Easy to moderate

Scenery:
Eno River, Orange County farmland

Exposure:
Shady

Solitude:
Road noise from nearby I-85

Trail surface:
Dirt, some gravel

Hiking time:
50 minutes

Access:
No fees or permits

Maps:
Occoneechee Natural Area Map available from Eno River State Park

Facilities:
None

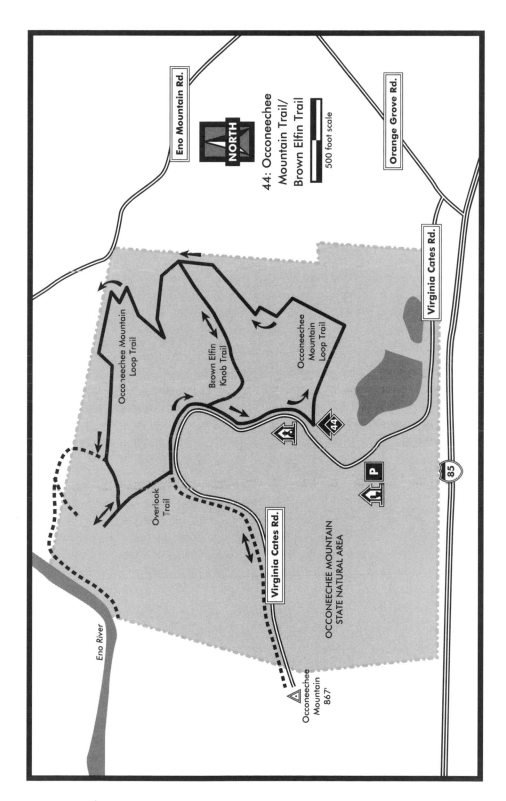

44: Occoneechee Mountain Trail/ Brown Elfin Trail

NORTH

500 foot scale

Eno Mountain Rd.

Orange Grove Rd.

Virginia Cates Rd.

85

Occoneechee Mountain Loop Trail

Brown Elfin Knob Trail

Occoneechee Mountain Loop Trail

44

P

Overlook Trail

Virginia Cates Rd.

Eno River

OCCONEECHEE MOUNTAIN STATE NATURAL AREA

Occoneechee Mountain 867'

geologists think that Occoneechee Mountain is all that remains of the peaks of an ancient Appalachian chain that ran through Orange County. Some call it "an Ice Age Outpost" because its north slope, rising up from the Eno River, creates a very cool microclimate. Among the plants out of their range are Bradley's spleenwort, mountain spleenwort, and climbing fern.

Traveling west from the Atlantic coast across the Piedmont in North Carolina, Occoneechee Mountain is the first indicator of the elevation increase ahead. At 867 feet, this small mountain rises 450 feet above the Eno River. To best appreciate Occoneechee Mountain, hike first through a pasture, down and to the right of the parking area. Never mind that all you hear is the drone of traffic on I-85. Soon you'll intersect Brown Elfin Knob Trail—named for the small, drab, brown butterfly often found in the area—on the left. Use it as an out-and-back walk up and over Brown Elfin Knob. The incredibly thick mountain laurel there blooms in late April.

When the Brown Elfin Knob Trail intersects the gravel road, reverse your path and return to the Occoneechee Mountain Loop to continue hiking there. Soon Hillsborough will come into view on your right.

Pass under the power line and climb the steep stairs to the left. You'll come to a false overlook; keep on going. Eventually you'll come to a serious cliff, made in part by the river but mostly by quarrying activity that dates back to the Civil War. Savor this view, because you'll have to travel many miles west to see anything else like it.

The trail soon intersects the gravel service road again. To hike to the summit, turn right. Once you reach the tower and check out the graffiti, return to the parking area via the gravel road.

The mountain has become a focus of conservation for several groups, including the Eno River Association, Eno State Park, and the nearby town of Hillsborough. The mountain was dedicated in 1999 as a State Natural Area and is now part of Eno River State Park. One unusual feature of the mountain area is a large deposit of pyrophyllite, a whitish, sometimes green, mineral that is used in the manufacture of ceramics.

Old Ebenezer Church/ Old Oak Ramble

←To Pittsboro
Wilsonville
64
To Raleigh,→
Cary, Apex
1008
45

IN BRIEF

Like the Seaforth Trail (see page 165), this hike has quick proximity to one of the swimming beaches at Jordan Lake. In addition, it passes by remnants of a church dating back to the 1700s, by several ponds, and through an oak grove.

DIRECTIONS

Ebenezer Church Recreation Area is 20 miles west of Raleigh on US 64 West, near Wilsonville. From Raleigh, turn left onto NC 1008 (this intersection is well marked). The entrance into the area is on your right, less than two miles from US 64. As you drive in, be sure to look for the white clapboard Ebenezer Church. (It'll be on your right.) This is the new building that replaced the old one you'll see along this hike.

After turning in, drive to the very last parking lot, near the beach. Park on the left on the far side of the lot; that's where you'll see the board marking the Old Ebenezer Church Trail.

DESCRIPTION

The first half of this hike, which begins on an old roadbed, passes by the remains of the old Ebenezer Church, which dates to the 1700s. Settled in the 1740s, the land in this area saw action in the Revolutionary War. You'll also walk past a small duck pond. As the trail traverses the pond dam, be sure to look for duck boxes. Also look for a quadruple-trunk oak tree.

KEY AT-A-GLANCE INFORMATION

Length:
2.5 miles
Configuration:
Lumpy barbell
Difficulty:
None
Scenery:
Historic church remains, ponds frequented by ducks, lots of species of oak trees
Exposure:
Shady
Solitude:
None on busy summer weekends
Trail surface:
Sand, pine needles, roots
Hiking time:
1.3 hours
Access:
Ebenezer Church Recreation Area requires a $4 per car fee during June, July, August, and weekends during April, May, and September.
Maps:
Available at the gate
Facilities:
Picnic tables, rest rooms, swimming, snack machines, grills, boat ramps
Special comments:
Though swimming is allowed, no lifeguard is on duty. Each loop trail is about 0.9 mile long.

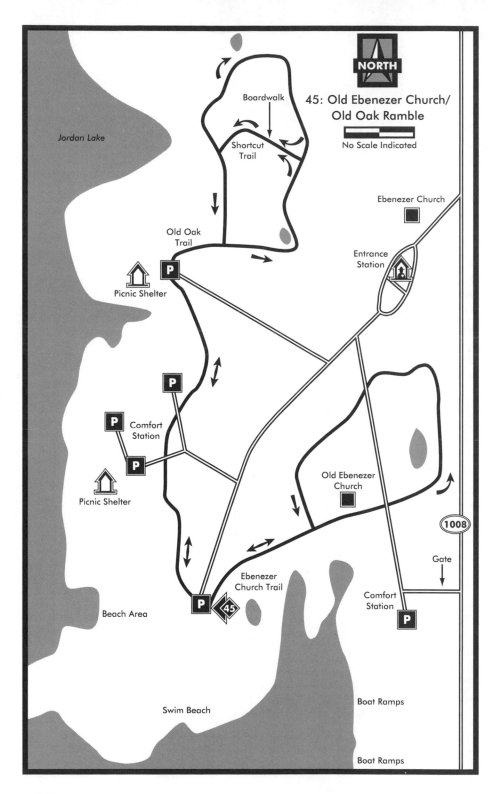

NORTH

45: Old Ebenezer Church/
Old Oak Ramble

No Scale Indicated

Jordan Lake

Boardwalk

Shortcut
Trail

Ebenezer Church

Old Oak
Trail

Entrance
Station

P

Picnic Shelter

P

P Comfort
Station

P

Picnic Shelter

Old Ebenezer
Church

1008

Gate

Comfort
Station

P

P 45

Beach Area

Ebenezer
Church Trail

Boat Ramps

Swim Beach

Boat Ramps

Building remains along the the Old Ebenezer Church Trail.

Though doubles are common and triples aren't exactly rare, a quadruple-trunk tree is a rarity. Be sure to note, too, the size of the pine trees back here. Rarely do you see pine trees growing this large.

After you complete this portion of the hike, you're ready to come out of the woods, cross the parking lot, and then head back into the woods. You'll know where to cross by looking for a crosswalk, near the entrance to this parking lot that seemingly disappears into the woods. When you're on the return trip, you'll see that this trail is called the "Beach Trail" (in this direction only).

When you reach the other loop hike, be sure to read the board about oak species. In no time you'll be able to distinguish between white oaks, red, oaks, post oaks, blackjack oaks, willow oaks, and water oaks!

As you walk this loop, at the very top you'll pass a pond that, during the cooler months, is home to several kinds of waterfowl, including mallards, buffleheads, pie-billed grebes, hooded mergansers, and scaups.

NEARBY ACTIVITIES
After the easy hike, take it even easier with a picnic on one of the 72 outdoor picnic tables in the area. There are grills and drinking water. Rest rooms are located at each of the three picnicking shelters. Shelter use is free unless a reservation is requested. Call the park office for more information at (919) 362-0586.

A bald eagle observation platform is located at the north end of Jordan Lake on NC 751.

Old Oxford Road

IN BRIEF

Lots of rarely seen, man-made history on this hike. Located in Duke Forest, this hike takes in part of the Old Oxford Road, which linked Oxford to Chapel Hill before Durham was established in 1867.

DIRECTIONS

From Raleigh, drive west on Interstate 40 to Chapel Hill. Exit onto US 15/501 North. Exit onto NC 751, turn left, and go underneath the bridge. Gate 2 is located on the right, directly across from Erwin Road. If you live in Chapel Hill, travel north on US 15/501 until you see the exit for NC 751.

DESCRIPTION

Hikes in Duke Forest provide Triangle-area residents with some great urban-escape exercise. Although storm damage from hurricanes, such as Fran in 1996, closed numerous trails, the parcels of the well-kept preserve offer over 30 miles of trails.

The 8,000 acres of Duke Forest, composed of farmland and forest purchased since the mid-1920s, are privately owned by Duke University.

The forest is the subject of numerous ongoing scientific endeavors by groups such as the School of Forestry at Duke. Public access and use is encouraged but limited to gated areas and designated trails.

KEY AT-A-GLANCE INFORMATION

Length:
3.2 miles

Configuration:
Loop, with spurs

Difficulty:
Easy

Scenery:
Research forests, cobblestone road more than 100 years old

Exposure:
Part shade/part sun

Solitude:
Busy; this path is popular with runners.

Trail surface:
Gravel road

Hiking time:
1.5 hours

Access:
No fees or permits

Maps:
Available at the Office of the Duke Forest; (919) 613-8013

Facilities:
None

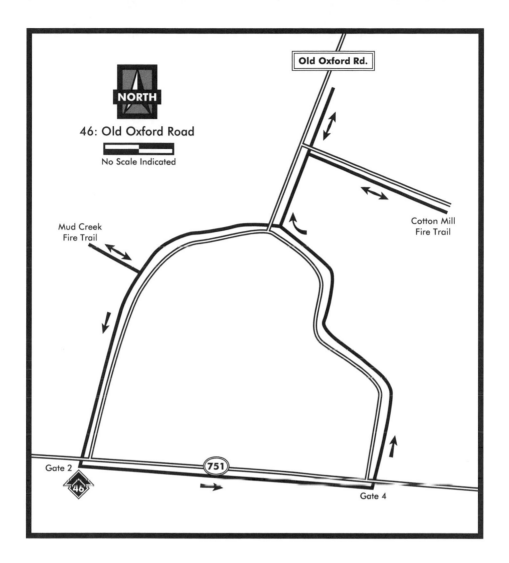

NORTH

46: Old Oxford Road

No Scale Indicated

Old Oxford Rd.

Mud Creek
Fire Trail

Cotton Mill
Fire Trail

Gate 2

46

751

Gate 4

The main part of this hike follows the road between Gate 2 and Gate 4 in Duke Forest. Between the two gates, you'll have three opportunities to add out-and-back hikes. From Gate 2, follow the gravel roadbed until it curves sharply to the left. At the curve, walk off the road, walking straight along a logging path into the woods. Soon you'll see a slatted wooden footbridge to the left. Walk to the footbridge. (This maneuver takes you back to the gravel road, avoiding a walk through private property.)

Your first opportunity to hike an out-and-back spur comes 0.6 mile into the hike. Turn right to hike along the Old Oxford Road. Be careful, though, because the bumpy nature of the cobblestones makes it easy to turn an ankle. (It also boggles the mind to think about how bumpy a carriage ride would have been over these stones.)

Not far up the Old Oxford Road you can turn to the right on yet another spur, this one the Cotton Mill Fire Trail. It, too, goes out-and-back for a total of 0.6 mile.

As you walk along this spur, be sure to note the shagbark oak trees.

When you return to the Old Oxford Road, turn right to walk to its conclusion. You'll know you're there when you see the parking lot for some apartments. Turn around and retrace your steps to the main road. Altogether, the Old Oxford Road and the Cotton Mill Fire Trail add 1.2 miles to the hike.

Once you're back on the main gravel road, hike right. Soon you'll see the Mud Creek Fire Trail. Turn right and hike out and back, adding another 0.4 mile to the total.

When you return to the main road, turn right and walk to the end, which is Gate 4. To return to your car, you can either hike left along NC 751 for 0.6 mile, or retrace your steps along the gravel road (1 mile). Hiking along NC 751 is a bit dicey, because people drive through here like their hair is on fire.

Pea Creek/ Dunnagan's Ramble

IN BRIEF

This easy loop hike begins with the Pea Creek Trail in the Cole Mill section of Eno River State Park. On the Pea Creek Trail, follow the river and pass by interesting rock formations. On the Dunnagan Trail portion of the hike, you'll pass by remnants of the dam used to create a reservoir for the Durham Pump Station and by the grave of Catharine Dunnagan.

DIRECTIONS

From Durham, travel west on Interstate 85. Exit onto Cole Mill Road. Just past the Eno River Bridge, turn left. Follow the road into the Cole Mill section. Park in the second parking area for the information station.

DESCRIPTION

From the parking lot, hike along the Pea Creek Trail, following the Eno River. After crossing under the Cole Mill Road Bridge, you'll see where the Pea Creek Loop begins to the left. You, however, will continue following the river. Not far beyond the split, you'll see several rock formations on your left. The first one resembles huge shark fins. A little farther up the river, you'll see a mini-version of Sentinel Rock in Yosemite National Park.

When you arrive at Pea Creek, cross it by either rock hopping or balancing your way on a bridge nearly ruined by storms. (Crossing the bridge looks more difficult

KEY AT-A-GLANCE INFORMATION

Length:
3.1 miles from the parking lot

Configuration:
Loop

Difficulty:
Easy

Scenery:
Interesting rocks, river views, Durham Pump Station, old graves

Exposure:
Shady

Solitude:
Moderate

Trail surface:
Dirt

Hiking time:
1.8 hours

Access:
No fees or permits

Maps:
Eno River State Park, Cole Mill Section

Facilities:
Rest rooms, water, picnic tables

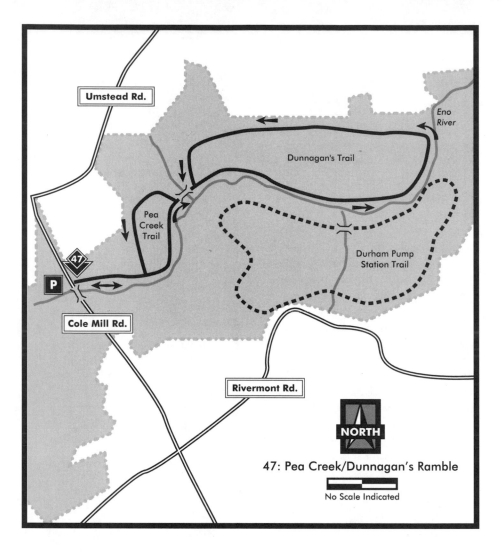

Umstead Rd.

Eno River

Dunnagan's Trail

Pea Creek Trail

47

P

Cole Mill Rd.

Durham Pump Station Trail

Rivermont Rd.

NORTH

47: Pea Creek/Dunnagan's Ramble

No Scale Indicated

than it really is.) Continue following the river. As you pass through a beech forest, be sure to note the sycamore trees that shade the river: Some of the tree roots, now exposed due to river erosion, curve like hair as they clutch the river bank.

As you cross the rock scramble, look across the river for the remnants of the dam built as part of the Durham Pump Station. If you look carefully, you'll see eroded concrete and steel rods. (This may be difficult when the trees are fully leafed.)

Almost immediately, the trail swings left; you'll ascend a gentle ridge along an old roadbed. After passing a huge, gnarly, shaggybark oak tree on the right, keep an eye out for the grave of Catharine Dunnagan, which will be on your left.

Dick Dunnagan of Beloit, Wisconsin, has made a study of the genealogy of Dunnagans in America. His work indicates that a Thomas Dunnagan lived in the area as early as 1752; other research conducted by Martha Gujda of Carlsbad, California, indicates the presence of

Dunnagans in the area as early as 1730. Oral tradition indicates that there was a Dunnagan's Mill on one of the creeks flowing into the Eno River, though the site has not yet been found. The grave is thought to be that of Catharine Link, who married Norman Dunnagan in 1854. Dunnagan family research indicates that Catharine lived to be a ripe 80 years old, quite an accomplishment for the time.

After passing the grave, you'll descend to Pea Creek. Cross the creek, and hike to the right along the remaining portion of the Pea Creek Trail. You'll ascend and descend a hill before returning to the original split.

Peninsula Trail

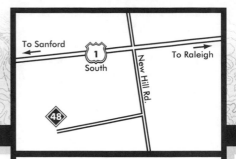

To Sanford ← 1 South → To Raleigh

New Hill Rd.

48

IN BRIEF

This easy lakeside walk, a composite of three relatively short trails, is still under development in Harris Lake County Park.

DIRECTIONS

From Raleigh: Travel south on US 1 to the New Hill exit. Turn left, and follow brown signs to Harris Lake County Park. The trail departs from the right side of the large parking area (near the picnic tables) located at the end of the road.

DESCRIPTION

Opened in 1999, Harris Lake is one of the newest and largest parks in Wake County. The lake is a reservoir for Carolina Power and Light's (CP&L) Harris Nuclear Power Plant. CP&L have made the park's land available to Wake County through a $1-a-year lease. The lake was built in the early 1980s to provide CP&L with a reservoir of water for the plant's cooling towers. The park occupies a peninsula-shaped area of Harris Lake. Following the Peninsula Trail along the edge of Harris Lake, you'll be hard-pressed not to take in two other trails, Beaver Loop Trail and White Tail Trail, that attach to the Peninsula Trail.

All three trails are blazed red, and it's hard to know exactly where one ends and another begins. The Peninsula Trail will likely undergo change in the future as Harris Lake County Park is further

KEY AT-A-GLANCE INFORMATION

Length:
3 miles, planned to be 5
Configuration:
Out-and-back
Difficulty:
Easy
Scenery:
Great for watching waterfowl
Exposure:
Filtered sun
Solitude:
Moderate
Trail surface:
Pine needles
Hiking time:
45 minutes
Access:
No fees or permits
Maps:
Harris Lake County Park
Facilities:
Rest rooms, playground, picnic area
Special comments:
Harris Park also contains a mountain bike trail, built and maintained in part by NC FATS. As much as you might want to hike this trail, please don't. Mountain bikers don't have many trails in the area to call their own. Besides, etiquette requires that walkers must yield to bikers.

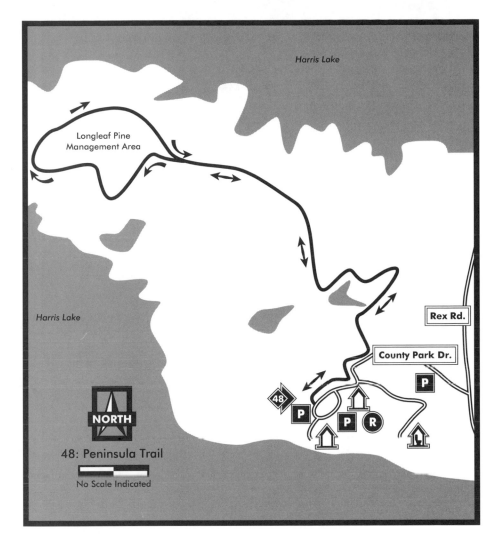

Harris Lake

Longleaf Pine
Management Area

Harris Lake

Rex Rd.

County Park Dr.

NORTH

48: Peninsula Trail

No Scale Indicated

developed. For now, however, you can enjoy a nice stroll among the pines, which are the stomping grounds of numerous birds. Watch for gnatcatchers, pine warblers, and common yellow throats in the summer. Waders can be found in the swampier margin areas of the lake. In winter, Bonaparte gulls are regulars at the lake.

A further buffer zone of 1,267 acres around the lake and plant is leased by CP&L to NC State University. NCSU's College of Forest Resources is conduct-

ing research and teaching on the tract while CP&L retains rights to timber revenue. Call the park at (919) 387-4342 for a map.

NEARBY ACTIVITIES
If you enjoyed the Peninsula Trail, take a look at what brought together the park area, lake, and trail: The Harris Nuclear Power Plant. The juxtaposition of nature with nuclear power is interesting and deserves a studied visit. The plant is located 22 miles southwest of Raleigh,

151

near the town of New Hill. A visitor's center is located near the plant on New Hill–Holleman Road. Follow the signs to the Harris Energy and Environmental Center. Activities at the center include an electricity learning lab hosted by "Sparky," the center's mascot. The White Oak Nature Trail features native plants and trees surrounding the power plant. The center is open 9 a.m. to 4 p.m., Monday through Friday. Call (919) 362-3261 for more information.

Penny's Bend Ridge and River Hike

IN BRIEF

A fine April afternoon and nothing to do? Then hike here, at Penny's Bend. The dirt here is more like that of the prairie than it is of North Carolina. According to people who know their dirt, there's nothing like this soil to be found elsewhere in the state. Because of the unusual turf, you can see wildflowers that just don't typically grow here. Plus, you can enjoy a fine walk across a meadow that is home to several bluebird houses.

DIRECTIONS

From Interstate 85 in Durham, travel north on Roxboro Road, turning right onto Old Oxford Highway. Turn left onto Snow Hill Road, just after passing over the Eno River Bridge. Turn left immediately into a small dirt parking area.

DESCRIPTION

The Eno River peninsula, which is Penny's Bend, is formed by the changes in direction of the river from east to south, east again, and then north. Pasture, hardwood forest, and a pond make this a short but diverse hike. Watch for a seven-trunk hackberry tree as you hike.

Before you start hiking, listen for the sound of the Eno River; you'll hear a lot of this as you hike along the River Bend Trail. Also, look for the remnants of Cameron's Mill, built in 1835, on the left as you leave the parking lot. If you're here in mid-spring, look for the wild

KEY AT-A-GLANCE INFORMATION

Length:
2.5 miles

Configuration:
Loop with a cut-through

Difficulty:
Easy

Scenery:
River views, wildflowers, field of cedar trees

Exposure:
Sunny across the ridge; shady in the woods

Solitude:
Moderate

Trail surface:
Dirt and grass

Hiking time:
45 minutes

Access:
No fees or permits

Maps:
Available at the Totten Center at the North Carolina Botanical Garden in Chapel Hill

Facilities:
None

Special comments:
The orange-blazed River Bend Trail is a 1.5-mile loop; the yellow-blazed Ridge Trail is 0.75 mile long.

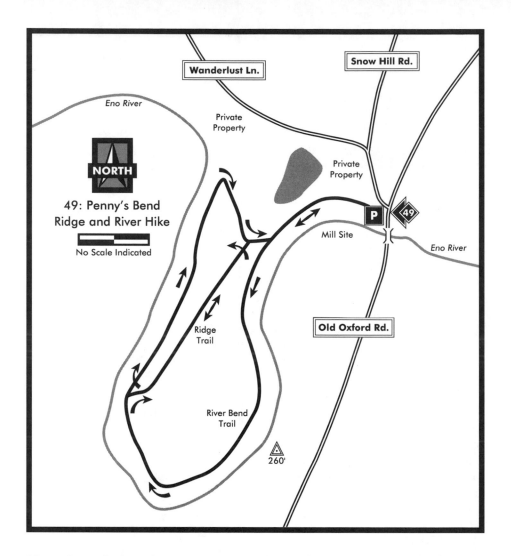

Map labels:
- Wanderlust Ln.
- Snow Hill Rd.
- Eno River
- Private Property
- Private Property
- NORTH
- 49: Penny's Bend Ridge and River Hike
- No Scale Indicated
- P
- 49
- Mill Site
- Eno River
- Ridge Trail
- Old Oxford Rd.
- River Bend Trail
- 260'

blue indigo, which rarely grows outside Illinois and Iowa, and for the larkspur, which is on the endangered species list. Also watch for the smooth purple-coneflower, a federally listed endangered species that grows in Penny's Bend's alkaline soil. (Because of the unique character of the soil and rare specimens of wildflowers found here, the Army Corps of Engineers asked the North Carolina Botanical Garden, located about 20 miles away in Chapel Hill, to manage the area.)

Although the two trails leave together from the upper right side of the parking lot, you'll very quickly have to choose which of the two trails to follow. My favorite way to hike these trails is to travel first along the river, then walk out and back across the ridge, and then come back to the River Bend Trail (the trail closest to the river) to continue following the river. When you cross the ridge, look for bluebirds.

NEARBY ACTIVITIES

Less than ten miles up Old Oxford Highway from Penny's Bend is the historic Stagville Center. This former estate comprises the remnants of one of the largest plantations of the pre–Civil War South. The plantation belonged to the Bennehan-Cameron family, whose combined holdings totalled approximately 900 slaves and almost 30,000 acres by 1860. Stagville offers a view of the past, especially that of its African-American community, by allowing visitors to guide themselves around its extensive grounds. In addition, Stagville offers the public many learning opportunities. The site is open Monday through Friday from 9 a.m. to 4 p.m. Call (919) 620-0120 for more information.

Raven Rock Loop

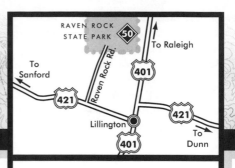

IN BRIEF

This hike winds through forest and slow-moving streams to Raven Rock. Raven Rock is a mile-long, 100-foot-high rock jutting out over the Cape Fear River. Yes, you need to make time to go see it, for it is truly the mother of all rock outcroppings in the Triangle.

DIRECTIONS

From Raleigh: Travel south on US 401 to Lillington. At the intersection of US 421 and US 401 in downtown Lillington, turn right onto US 421. Follow the signs to Raven Rock State Park. Trails begin from the left, center, and right of the parking lot. Raven Rock Loop begins to the right of the parking lot.

DESCRIPTION

Often hailed by area hikers as the most popular trail in Raven Rock State Park, this hike can be lengthened to a over three miles by continuing around the Little Creek Loop, which begins at the Raven Rock overlook.

The bedrock in the area was formed over 400 million years ago and the fury of wind and water is responsible for the carving of the magnificent Raven Rock formation.

Once called Patterson's Rock (for Gilbert Patterson, a farmer living in Buies Creek who capsized his canoe in the area and struggled ashore near the huge rock outcropping), this outstanding

KEY AT-A-GLANCE INFORMATION

Length:
2.1 miles

Configuration:
Loop

Difficulty:
Moderate

Scenery:
Excellent views of the Cape Fear River

Exposure:
Filtered sun

Solitude:
Very busy on weekends

Trail surface:
Dirt

Hiking time:
1.5 hours

Access:
No fees or permits

Maps:
Raven Rock State Park

Facilities:
Rest rooms, water, picnic tables, snack machines

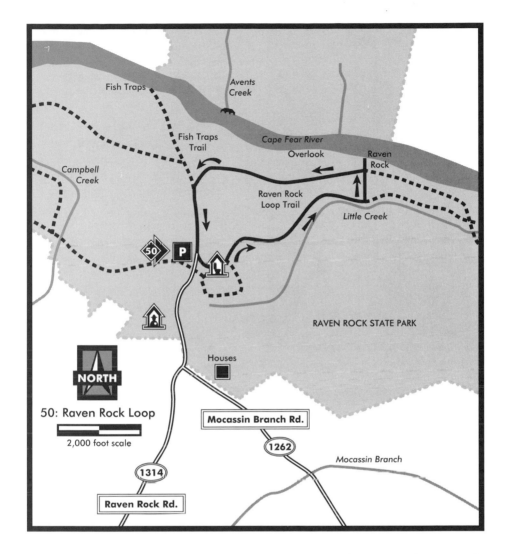

50: Raven Rock Loop

2,000 foot scale

RAVEN ROCK STATE PARK

Fish Traps

Avents Creek

Fish Traps Trail

Cape Fear River

Overlook

Raven Rock

Campbell Creek

Raven Rock Loop Trail

Little Creek

Houses

Mocassin Branch Rd.

1262

Mocassin Branch

1314

Raven Rock Rd.

rock outcropping later became known as Raven Rock. Some say it was for the ravens seen roosting here, although other historians say it was for Raven, the son of Hancock, a Tuscarora chief.

Be sure to walk down the spiraling wooden stairs to the base of Raven Rock to observe the action of water undercutting this huge rock. Also take the camera for the obligatory shot back up the rock. (The stairs leading down are a deck builder's fantasy!) Here, a stone balcony looks out over the river and its flood plain. My friend Tracie says this is one of the best hikes around, especially in the spring, when the mountain laurel, which grows over the rock, blooms. Return to the trailhead by continuing around the loop.

If you want to make an overnighter out of the hike, there is a year-round family wilderness campground located on the Campbell Creek Loop Trail, which is accessed from the same trailhead as the Raven Rock Loop. The site is approximately 2.5 miles from the

Towering Raven Rock.

parking area. There are five camp-sites with fire circles, tent pads, and an outdoor toilet. Obtain a camping permit from the park office. Call (910) 893-4888 for more information.

The park also offers regularly scheduled educational programs and hikes. Contact the park office at the number above for more information on these programs.

Ridge Trail/
Shakori Ramble

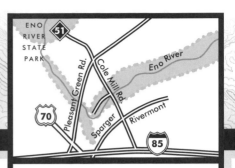

IN BRIEF
Looking for hiking solitude? Here's your hike. The trails are relatively new and not many people know about them.

DIRECTIONS
From Durham, travel west on Interstate 85. Exit onto US 70 West. Almost immediately, turn right onto Pleasant Green Road. Turn left onto Cole Mill Road; follow it until it ends in Eno River State Park. From the first parking area (on the right, unmarked) follow the signs that say River Access Trails.

DESCRIPTION
To begin this hike, walk first along Buck-quarter Creek Trail, using the upper path (away from the river). At about three-quarters of a mile along the Buckquarter Creek Trail, you'll see the signs marking the Ridge Trail, leaving on the right. Follow this trail, crossing a tiny creek near an abandoned cabin. This cabin belonged to the Martin family, who lived here from 1908 to 1920. Soon you'll come to Buckquarter Creek, which can be traversed either by rock hopping, by wading, or by walking across any one of a number of large, downed trees that have fallen across the creek.

Just past Buckquarter Creek, you'll see the Shakori Trail on the right. Native American Eno, Shakori, and Occonee-chee tribes lived along the Eno River prior to colonial settlement. You can

KEY AT-A-GLANCE INFORMATION

Length:
4.3 miles

Configuration:
Balloon

Difficulty:
Moderate

Scenery:
Just woods

Exposure:
Shady

Solitude:
Very quiet

Trail surface:
Pine needles and leaves

Hiking time:
1.5 hours

Access:
No fees or permits

Maps:
Hand-drawn supplement to the Eno River State Park map, available from the Eno River State Park Office

Facilities:
Rest rooms and water at the park office

Special comments:
Be prepared to ford a major creek until a bridge is built!

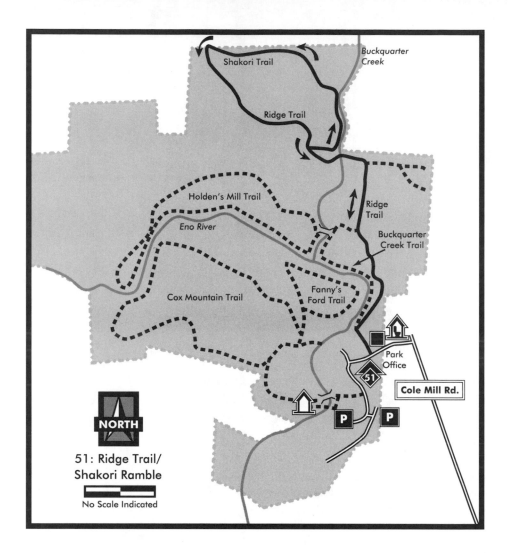

**51: Ridge Trail/
Shakori Ramble**

No Scale Indicated

either hike right along the Shakori Trail, which has a more gentle grade, or continue along the Ridge Trail, which requires a more constant push up the ridge. In either case, the trails intersect at the northern boundary of the park and can be hiked in a loop.

If you bring your fishing pole and your valid North Carolina fishing license, you can cast for your dinner in the Eno. Roanoke bass and catfish are two of many types of fish in the river. If you bring your canoe, a launch point is available in the parking area of this hike's trailhead. If you bring your swim trunks, leave them in the car since swimming is not allowed. For a picnic after the hike, the Few's Ford access area contains a riverside picnic site with two tables. More tables and grills are located beyond the parking lot. Call the park at (919) 383-1686 for more information.

NEARBY ACTIVITIES

If you plan to visit the Eno River State Park during the Fourth of July holiday, be aware that thousands head to the park each year for the annual Festival for the Eno. The festival is three days of bluegrass music, clogging, and tale spinning. Craft booths and a food court round out the experience. By some estimates, the Eno River Festival is the largest Fourth of July gathering in the state.

Sal's Branch/ Pott's Branch/ Oak Rock Ramble

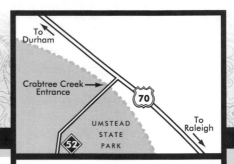

To Durham

Crabtree Creek Entrance

70

UMSTEAD
STATE
PARK

52

To Raleigh

IN BRIEF

Along the way, you'll see remnants of stone bridges built to prevent erosion when the land was used for farming as well as remnants of the old picnic area. You'll also notice several beech trees that have been carved and, if you hike in the early spring, small patches of daffodils planted by the families who once lived here.

DIRECTIONS

From Raleigh: Drive west on US 70 as if you're going to the airport. You'll see the left turn for the Crabtree Creek Section of Umstead State Park before you reach the airport.

Once inside the gate, drive all the way to the end and park in the very last parking lot. (Turn neither left nor right on other park roads.) You'll see the Sal's Branch Trail on the right side of the parking lot, at the end.

DESCRIPTION

The Sal's Branch Trail is where my friend Thresa earned her nickname, "Snakecharmer." Thresa has an uncanny ability to draw snakes to a trail, and her talent typically gives me just enough of an adrenaline rush to get to the end of the hike. Regardless of the snake potential, this is a great hike for just about anybody.

Hike first along the Sal's Branch Trail (blazed with an orange circle), which

KEY AT-A-GLANCE INFORMATION

Length:
Sal's Branch loop is 2.2 miles, Pott's Branch Loop is 0.75 miles, and Oak Rock Loop is 1 mile. Total mileage is 3.95 miles.

Configuration:
1 balloon and 2 loops

Difficulty:
Moderate

Scenery:
Old roadbeds, remnants of stone bridges, and picnic grills

Exposure:
Shady

Solitude:
None; even if there are no people out, you'll still hear tremendous noise coming from RDU Airport. That tremble you feel isn't your pulse: It's a 737 taking off.

Trail surface:
Pine needles, dirt, some patches of quartz gravel, roots

Hiking time:
2.4 hours

Access:
No fees or permits

Maps:
Umstead State Park

Facilities:
Rest rooms, water, picnic tables, canoe rental

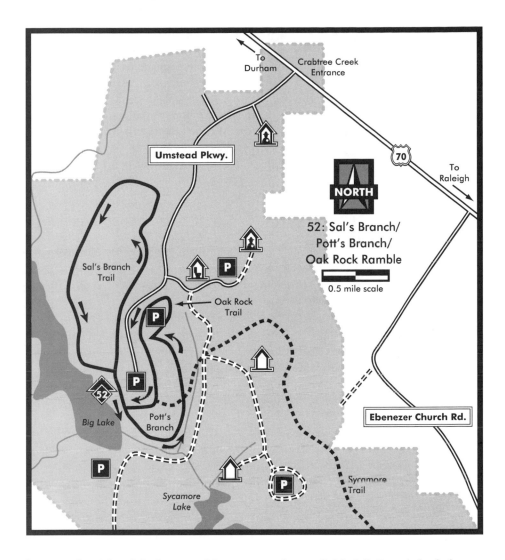

To Durham

Crabtree Creek
Entrance

Umstead Pkwy.

70

To Raleigh

NORTH

52: Sal's Branch/
Pott's Branch/
Oak Rock Ramble

0.5 mile scale

Sal's Branch
Trail

P

Oak Rock
Trail

P

P

52

Big Lake

Pott's
Branch

Ebenezer Church Rd.

P

Sycamore
Trail

P

Sycamore
Lake

leaves to the right of the lower parking lot. This easy, 2.2-mile balloon circles close to the entrance road and then, later, around Big Lake. Rowboats and canoes are available for rent on the lake.

Along the way you'll see remnants of stone walls built by farmers, as well as the Civilian Conservation Corps (CCC), in the days before the area was a state park. As you near Big Lake, you'll pass through one of the original picnic areas. The stone grills you see were built in the late 1930s and early 1940s.

As you finish Sal's Branch, look for a metal post marking the beginning of the Pott's Branch Trail (blazed with an orange diamond). It's on the right, about halfway up the hill to the parking area. The loop hike will add another three-quarters of a mile to your hike. The only tricky part occurs when the trail intersects the Sycamore Trail. Instead of climbing the stairs to your left, just keep walking straight. Pott's Branch will follow the creek just a little more before turning up the hill to the left.

Tall pines at the beginning of Sal's Branch.

As you ascend the hill through a picnic area, look for the Oak Rock Trail (blazed with a white square) on your right. This easy, one-mile loop serves as an interpretive nature trail. Along the way, you'll see signs identifying various trees.

After you finish walking the Oak Rock Trail, rejoin the upper loop of Pott's Branch Trail near the upper parking lot to return to the lower parking lot.

Seaforth Trail

IN BRIEF

Like a little beach time with your hiking? If so, this is the hike for you. Before or after enjoying the rays at Seaforth Beach, you can stroll among the woods, look for trolls in the area's best hollow-trunk tree, and traverse a swamp via a boardwalk, all while enjoying a breeze that blows across the peninsula where this recreation area is located.

DIRECTIONS

From Raleigh: Seaforth Recreation Area is about 28 miles away on US 64 West. Look for signs pointing to the left after you cross the second Jordan Lake bridge. Once inside the gate, drive to the last parking lot. The trailhead is across the parking lot from the last rest room. As you study the map, note that the trail doesn't make a complete loop. When you reach the end, you'll be at one of the first picnic shelters you passed on the way in. It is, however, no trouble to walk left, back to the trailhead.

DESCRIPTION

This day-use area is home to Jordan Lake's longest swim beach at 1,100 feet. The beach slopes gradually into the water and is a nice place to swim after a hike. If you're still bursting with energy after a hike and a swim, check out the sand volleyball court.

Just after starting this trail, look for the area's best hollow-trunk tree. Both the

KEY AT-A-GLANCE INFORMATION

Length:
1.5 miles
Configuration:
Loop
Difficulty:
None
Scenery:
Mixed hardwoods, maybe snakes, lake views through the trees
Exposure:
Part sun/part shade
Solitude:
Boat noise on the weekends
Trail surface:
Sand, roots, boardwalk
Hiking time:
30 minutes
Access:
Seaforth Recreation Area requires a $4 per car entrance fee during June, July, and August and on weekends during April, May, and September.
Maps:
Check the board at the trailhead
Facilities:
Picnic tables, rest rooms, swimming beaches, snack machines, grills, boat ramps
Special comments:
As one of the area's most popular lakeshore beaches, this area will be crowded on weekends.

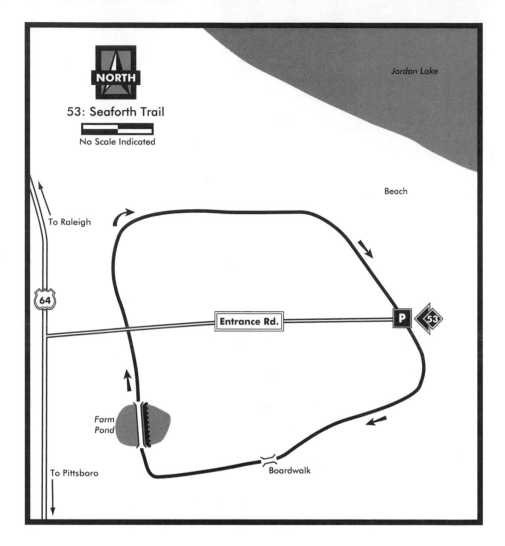

53: Seaforth Trail

No Scale Indicated

To Raleigh

Jordan Lake

Beach

64

Entrance Rd.

P 53

Farm Pond

To Pittsboro

Boardwalk

tree and the hollow trunk are so large that it's hard to believe that the tree is still standing! And it's really easy to imagine that at night, on a full moon, little trolls come out to dance in the moonlight.

Farther up the trail, you'll come to an extensive boardwalk. If you hike here in summer, look for blooming hibiscus, which is a leftover from the days when the area was farmland. After walking the boardwalk, you'll come to a set of stone steps that permit you to walk across the dam of a farm pond. Note how much

smaller this farm pond is than it once was.

Eventually the trail bends, crosses the entrance road, and re-enters the woods. Birds you may see include brown-headed nuthatches and pine warblers. From here, you're on the home stretch, and the only serious hiking trouble you'll have is if people at the picnic shelters are grilling hamburgers! If they are, you might want to try out your Yogi the Bear skills.

There are 47 picnic tables scattered around the area, along with some 28 grills. There are boat launches here but no boat rentals. Fishing is allowed anywhere along the shoreline, except in the swimming area. For more information, contact the park office at (919) 362-0586.

NEARBY ACTIVITIES

Of special interest to visitors in this area is the North Carolina Wildlife Resources Commission bald eagle observation platform, located on the north end of Jordan Lake. To reach the platform, return to US 64 and turn right. Turn left on NC 751. The platform will be on the left side of the road.

Boardwalk on the Seaforth Trail.

Shelley Lake Loop with Bent Creek Spur

IN BRIEF

This trail may be the most popular greenway walk in Raleigh. It passes the Shelley Lake "beach," a grassy area where locals come out to get a "lake bake," in the summer, do some serious people watching, or play Frisbee. Several spokes are attached to the basic loop so that you can add more mileage to your outing.

DIRECTIONS

In Raleigh: Go to Shelley Lake, which is located on Millbrook Road, between North Hills Drive and Lead Mine Road. Park in the lot below the dam. From the parking lot at the Shelley Lake Dam, go underneath Millbrook Road.

DESCRIPTION

Begin the Shelley Lake hike at the parking lot at the bottom of the dam. Walk up the hill, and pass Shelley Beach and the soccer fields. The trail enters the woods, where you'll soon see the Snelling Branch Greenway come in on the right. Snelling Branch is a part of the Lead Mine Creek Greenway. The trail links Shelley Lake with Optimist Park. After crossing a wooden bridge that crosses a tributary of Lead Mine Creek, a short side trail leads to a playground on the right. Back on the Snelling Branch Trail, it leaves the creek, crosses through a wooded area, and emerges near the ballfields of Optimist Park. The out-and-back walk on the greenway adds a mile.

KEY AT-A-GLANCE INFORMATION

Length:
5.4 miles

Configuration:
Balloon

Difficulty:
Easy

Scenery:
Average

Exposure:
Mostly sunny

Solitude:
None

Trail surface:
Asphalt

Hiking time:
1.5 hours

Access:
No fees or permits

Maps:
Capital Area Greenway Trail System Map or Raleigh Bike Map

Facilities:
Rest rooms, pedal boats, picnic tables

Special comments:
This hike is composed of the 2.2-mile Shelley Lake Loop and the 2.2-mile out-and-back walk along Bent Creek Greenway. It also includes the 1-mile out-and-back walk along Snelling Branch Greenway.

168

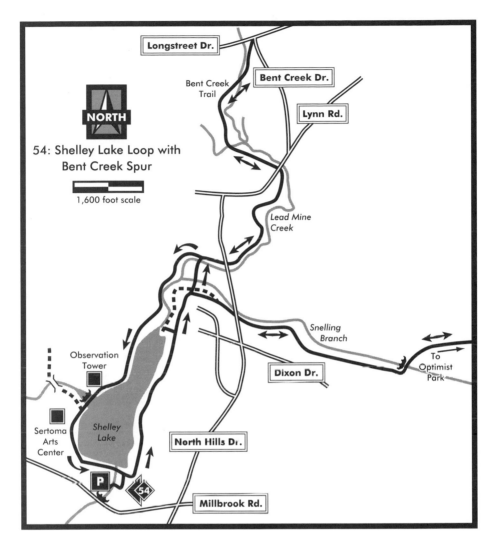

NORTH

54: Shelley Lake Loop with Bent Creek Spur

1,600 foot scale

Longstreet Dr.

Bent Creek Dr.

Bent Creek Trail

Lynn Rd.

Lead Mine Creek

Snelling Branch

Dixon Dr.

To Optimist Park

Observation Tower

Sertoma Arts Center

Shelley Lake

North Hills Dr.

P 54

Millbrook Rd.

Retrace your steps and return to the Shelley Lake Loop. Just a short distance up the path you'll see the Bent Creek Branch going off the top of the Shelley Lake Loop. This greenway is one of the nicest in Raleigh and the out-and-back will add another 2.2 miles to your hike. The trail first heads east through a tunnel under North Hills Drive, then turns north along a sanitary sewer easement to Lynn Road. You can stay on the paved Bent Creek Trail and continue on through a stand of river birch trees. The

trail crosses Lead Mine Creek and heads east to again cross the creek. The Bent Creek Trail ends at the intersection of Bent Creek and Longstreet Drives.

Again, retrace your steps back to the Shelley Lake Loop. After passing the Bent Creek intersection, the Shelley Lake Loop turns back toward the Sertoma Arts Center and the picnic areas. After passing the boat rental shed, you'll return to the parking lot below the dam.

Shelley Lake is a popular spot for hikers as well as bikers and skaters. There have been reports of attacks on trail users in the past in this area, so be mindful of your safety and take precautions such as hiking with others.

Throughout the year, the Sertoma Arts Center offers continuing education classes, plus the lake is home to a pedal boat concession that runs March through November. Soccer fields, on the right side of the lake, are often busy. You're likely to see cyclists, in-line skaters, and joggers any time during the year; cross–country skiers come here in the winter when there's snow. But April and May are probably the best times to sample this wonderful trail; it seems that everyone in the Triangle comes out at that time to welcome the good weather back to the area.

Shepherd Nature Trail

IN BRIEF

This is a self-guided nature trail in Duke Forest. In addition to the original interpretive signs explaining natural and man-made features, the trail has signs showing how a forest recovers from storm damage.

DIRECTIONS

From Raleigh, drive west on Interstate 40 to Chapel Hill. Exit onto US 15/501 North. Drive US 15/501, taking the bypass around Durham. Exit north onto NC 751, turn left, and go underneath the bridge. Shepherd Nature Trail is located on the right, 1.2 miles from US 15/501. Park at Gate C, which is tucked up in the woods.

DESCRIPTION

This hike, located in the Durham Division of Duke Forest, is a good one to take if you'd like to see the positive side of storm damage. In sections along this trail, up to 80% of the canopy trees were blown down during Hurricane Fran in 1996. You'll quickly see how a canopy gap, the large opening left when a storm breaks out the tops of trees, helps a forest to recover. In addition, the interpretive hike takes you through a typical North Carolina Piedmont environment of bottomland forest and rocky hilltops.

Duke Forest is composed of 8,000 acres of land owned by Duke University. The public is welcome but must use only

KEY AT-A-GLANCE INFORMATION

Length:
Just under a mile

Configuration:
Balloon

Difficulty:
Easy

Scenery:
Forest areas both touched and untouched by severe storms

Exposure:
Part shade/part sun

Solitude:
Busy

Trail surface:
Wood chips, dirt, roots, rocks

Hiking time:
40 minutes

Access:
No fees or permits

Maps:
Brochure available at the trailhead

Facilities:
None

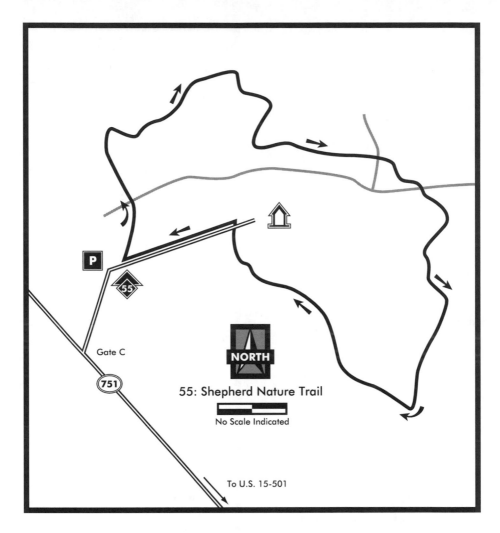

55: Shepherd Nature Trail

No Scale Indicated

To U.S. 15-501

those areas designated as public access. The forest is home to numerous forestry-related scientific endeavors, and it is open for hiking only during daylight hours. Mountain biking is not allowed on the Shepherd Nature Trail but is allowed on the wider gravel forest roads.

From the gravel parking area, walk up a small hill until you see a homey picnic table and stone grill beneath some tall oaks. The trail, marked with a block of wood blazed with a white evergreen tree, departs to the left. Near the sign indicating that this trail was the Eagle

Scout project of Aaron Dornback in 1995, you'll find an interpretive brochure. The hike winds up and down several hills and crosses three streams.

The trail traverses land that was farmed by the Shepherd family until the 1920s, when Duke University bought it for use as a teaching forest. If you look hard along the way, you'll find evidence of furrows and rows, as well as a tiny rock wall marking a spot where an underground spring comes to the surface. Twenty-nine small wooden signs with a white tree outline also explain what tree snags are (those dead, leafless trees, typically sporting broken crowns) and how soil is made. Follow the markers to stay on the trail. Since hiking here, I have better understood epicormic branching, a term referring to how trees sprout to compensate for their broken tops.

There is a picnic shelter at the end of the trail. To reserve it, contact the Office of the Duke Forest at (919) 613-8013. A map of the Duke Forest is also available from the office.

Summit Trail/ Dam Site Combo

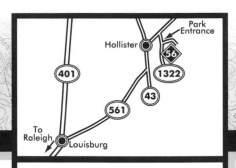

Map labels: Park Entrance, Hollister, 56, 401, 1322, 43, 561, To Raleigh, Louisburg

IN BRIEF

Looking for a quiet place away from the maddening crowds to do a little hiking? Then try this hike, located in Medoc Mountain State Park. In addition to scaling a granite ridge, you can walk along land that was once cultivated for grapes.

DIRECTIONS

Drive 25 miles north from Raleigh on US 401 to Louisburg. In Louisburg, turn right on NC 561 and travel another 30 miles to Hollister. In Hollister, follow the signs to Medoc Mountain State Park. Do not turn in at the first entrance you see, unless you're looking for a bathroom. The Summit/Dam Site Combo is located on the other side of the park. Follow the signs and turn in at the second entrance, which will be to your left. Look for a trail board behind the ranger office. That's where the trailhead is.

DESCRIPTION

Named by Sidney Weller, who cultivated grapes here and is credited with establishing the American system of grape culture, Medoc Mountain is named in honor of the Medoc province of the Bordeaux region of France. The short trails in this park have benches scattered along their length.

After walking through a pine thicket, you'll come to the top of the loop. I suggest hiking to the left, since doing so will let you hike the easy part of this hike last.

KEY AT-A-GLANCE INFORMATION

Length:
4 miles

Configuration:
Figure 8

Difficulty:
Moderate; elevation gain of 325 feet

Scenery:
Creeks, remnants of old dams, lots of quartz rocks typical of the land near the fall line between the coastal and Piedmont sections of the state

Exposure:
Mostly shady

Solitude:
You're apt to be alone here.

Trail surface:
White quartz, pine needles, roots

Hiking time:
1.25 hours

Access:
No fees or permits

Maps:
Available at the ranger station

Facilities:
Not on this side of the park

Special comments:
Rabies has been found in animals that live in the park; beware of any raccoons you might see.

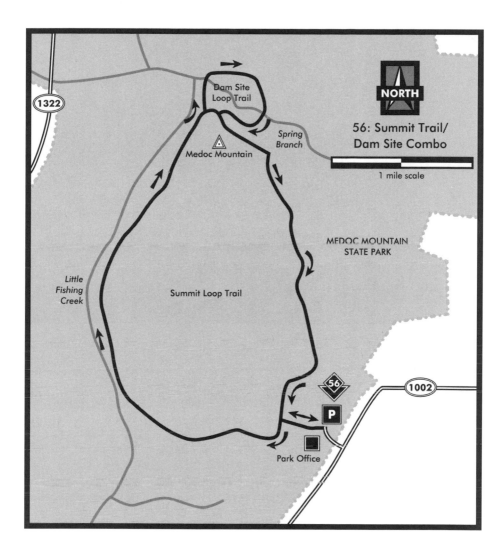

NORTH

56: Summit Trail/
Dam Site Combo

1 mile scale

MEDOC MOUNTAIN
STATE PARK

Dam Site
Loop Trail

Spring
Branch

Medoc Mountain

Little
Fishing
Creek

Summit Loop Trail

Park Office

1322

1002

56

P

Quickly the trail descends to Little Fishing Creek; along the way you might see an interpretive sign or two, pointing out running cedar or, more curiously, mountain laurel! It's very unusual to see these plants this far east.

As you walk along enjoying views of the creek, be sure to keep an eye to the right for glimpses of the granite ridge that forms Medoc Mountain. It's all that remains of a mountain range formed 350 million years ago by volcanic action. If you come to the Dam Site sign and haven't seen the granite ridge, take a

moment to retrace your steps and look up, now to your left, to see it.

The Dam Site Loop can be hiked either to the right or left, effectively turning these two loop trails into a figure 8. I recommend hiking to the right. Though you have an immediate push up, it doesn't last long. When the Dam Site Loop splits to the left, follow it along a high old roadbed and pass two sets of remains of dams. Soon the trail will loop back around to the sign, whereupon you'll push up the hill again. This time, stay to the right to come to the forested summit

175

Dam remains in Medoc Mountain State Park.

of Medoc Mountain. In the 1920s, this area was home to a Boy Scout camp.

To complete the hike, walk to the right along the old roadbed. Be sure to look for an old graveyard to your left near the end of the hike.

There are three group campsites in the park, each able to accommodate 30 people. The picnic shelter has a rest room with a couple of dozen picnic tables nearby. There are no hookups in the campsites, but there is a rest room. Camping is available from March 15 through November 30. Call the park office at (919) 362-1621 for more information.

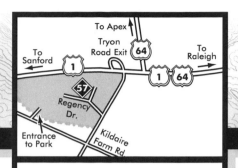

Symphony Lake

IN BRIEF

The woods around Symphony Lake are often alive with the sound of music! Why? Because, the North Carolina Symphony hold outdoor concerts here. Other times it may be because people are humming a happy tune as they walk around this lake.

DIRECTIONS

From Raleigh: Drive to Cary on US 64 West/US 1 South. Take the Tryon Road exit where US 64 and US 1 split, south of Cary. Loop underneath the Beltline. Turn right into Regency Park, and drive to where the road splits to loop the lake. Parking can be found in the lots of near-by office buildings.

DESCRIPTION

This is a very pleasant walk, especially after you're away from the top of the lake, where traffic enters Regency Park. When you hike here, keep an eye open for waterfowl. The first time I hiked this path I was lucky enough to see, tucked under a rather large shrub, a swan nesting. On other occasions, I've spotted mallards and paddling geese.

The greenway has been closed for renovations but is scheduled to reopen in April 2001. Renovations will include a resurfacing and widening of the trail to ten feet. Drainage improvements and benches will also be added. To check on the status of the greenway, call the Cary

KEY AT-A-GLANCE INFORMATION

Length:
1.2 miles

Configuration:
Loop

Difficulty:
Easy

Scenery:
Lake views

Exposure:
Sunny in the mornings

Solitude:
Busy

Trail surface:
Asphalt

Hiking time:
30 minutes

Access:
No fees or permits

Maps:
Cary Greenway Map

Facilities:
None

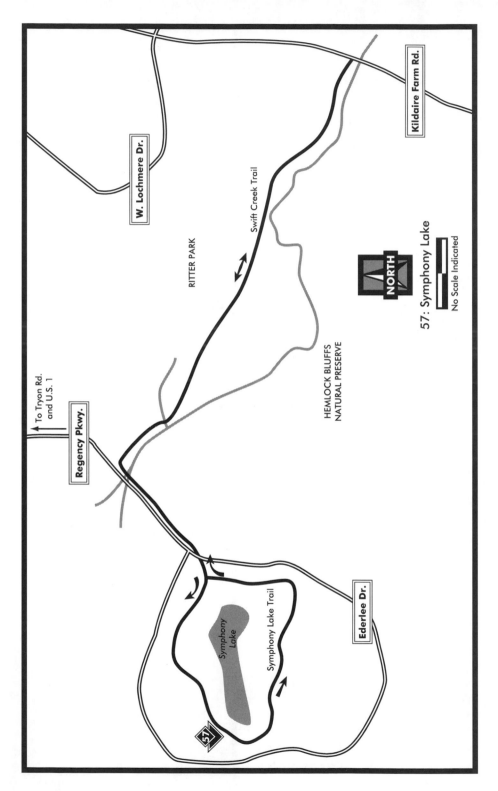

RITTER PARK

W. Lochmere Dr.

Kildaire Farm Rd.

Swift Creek Trail

To Tryon Rd.
and U.S. 1

Regency Pkwy.

HEMLOCK BLUFFS
NATURAL PRESERVE

NORTH

57: Symphony Lake

No Scale Indicated

Symphony
Lake

Symphony Lake Trail

Ederlee Dr.

57

Parks and Recreation department at (919) 469-4061. For information on the annual Fourth of July concert at Symphony Lake, call (919) 733-2750.

To lengthen this short hike by 1.6 miles, look for the Swift Creek Trail, which branches to the right off of Regency Parkway near the lake. Swift Creek is a 0.8-mile, asphalt-surfaced, out-and-back trail connecting Regency Parkway and Kildaire Farm Road. A spur on the left side of the trail (while headed toward Kildaire Farm Road) leads to Ritter Park. Area birders enjoy the small park for its numerous species of warblers.

NEARBY ACTIVITIES

The Hemlock Bluffs Nature Preserve lies south of the Swift Creek Trail. The 150-acre site contains north-facing bluffs along the creek. The bluffs contribute to a microclimate that is wetter and cooler than surrounding areas, supporting numerous plants uncommon to the Piedmont, including eastern hemlocks. To access the preserve from Symphony Lake, turn right on Tryon Road, then right again on Kildaire Farm Road. The preserve will appear on your right. Parking is located near the Stevens Nature Center, which you'll want to visit.

Inside the preserve, there are three trails. There is a Swift Creek Loop Trail (different from the Swift Creek Trail, which is north of the preserve on the other side of Swift Creek), which is less than a mile long. The trail loops through the floodplain area of Swift Creek and includes a system of boardwalks. The Beech Tree Cove Trail is less than a half-mile in length and features a large American beech. The Chestnut Oak Trail, 1.1 miles, loops through a hardwood forest. There is an observation deck along the north section of this trail.

To arrange a tour of the preserve, call (919) 387-5980.

CLEMMONS EDUCATIONAL
STATE FOREST

To
Garner

Old US 70

70

58

To
Goldsboro

Talking Trees Trail

IN BRIEF

If you have kids, or are—like me—easily
amused, you have to take this hike in
Clemmons Educational State Forest.
There's nowhere else in the Triangle
where the trees will talk to you, telling
you a little about themselves.

DIRECTIONS

From Raleigh: Drive east on US 70.
Brown signs point the way to Clemmons Educational State Forest, which is
about five miles southeast of Garner on
Old US 70.

DESCRIPTION

Located in the transitional area between
North Carolina's coastal plain and the
Piedmont in Johnston County, this forest
experience is a nice half-day trip with the
kids. You can camp as well as hike here,
but the majority of visitors are school
groups on daytrips. The forest is operated
by the state, but it is not a state park. It is
one of six Educational State Forests in
North Carolina, each with its own talking
trees trail. The 350 acres the forest occupies was claimed by the federal government during the depression, after the
forest was abandoned by farmers. The
Civilian Conservation Corp (CCC), a
productive and timely make-work program for the unemployed, placed a camp
on the land for CCC workers.

At the parking lot, walk down any of
the trails that weave in and out of the

KEY AT-A-GLANCE
INFORMATION

Length:
0.8 mile

Configuration:
Loop

Difficulty:
Easy

Scenery:
Talking trees

Exposure:
Mostly shaded

Solitude:
Most likely none

Trail surface:
Pine needles

Hiking time:
30 minutes

Access:
No fees or permits

Maps:
Available at the office on the way in

Facilities:
Rest rooms, water, picnic tables

Special comments:
This trail is wheelchair accessible.

180

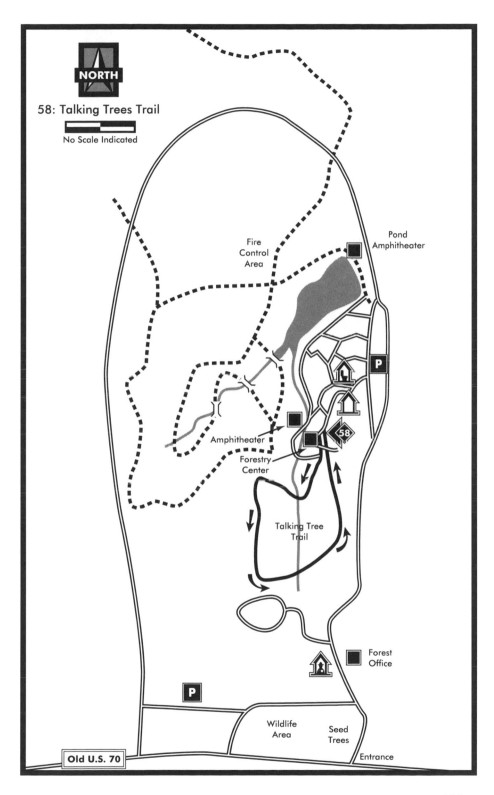

NORTH

58: Talking Trees Trail

No Scale Indicated

Fire Control Area

Pond Amphitheater

P

Amphitheater

Forestry Center

58

Talking Tree Trail

Forest Office

P

Wildlife Area

Seed Trees

Entrance

Old U.S. 70

181

picnic area. As you do, make your way to the left, to the Forest Center. The green-blazed Talking Tree Trail, funded in part by Carolina Power and Light, is to the left of the center.

As you walk, be sure to push the buttons and let the trees introduce themselves and tell you a little about what they do for us. Along the way, you'll meet a yellow poplar, a dogwood, an eastern red cedar, a white cedar, and several pine trees.

After experiencing talking trees, what's to stop you from experiencing the talking rocks? Similar to the Talking Trees Trail, the Forest Geology Trail features talking rocks. There are seven talking rocks, each with a 60-second message. Children learn how the rock was formed, its uses, and its economic significance in North Carolina.

If you want more than the self-guided tour, specially trained rangers are standing by at the forest to conduct tours and programs. The 30-minute programs layer education about the forest environment with practical skills such as math. Role playing and hands-on experiments help youngsters to retain information. Call the forest office at (919) 553-5651 for more information on tours and programs. The forest is open from mid-March through late November and is closed on Mondays. Admission is free.

NEARBY ACTIVITIES

If talking trees don't wet your whistle, then maybe a stop at the Coffee Mill will. Located in the heart of Clayton on Lombard Street, just off of US 70, the Coffee Mill provides a relaxing, environment for a cup of joe, a light breakfast, lunch, and desserts. For summer months, iced and frozen drinks such as smoothies and shakes are available. The Coffee Mill's phone number is (919) 550-0174.

Vista Point Recreation Area

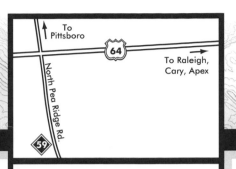

IN BRIEF

Of the three hikes at Lake Jordan included in this book, this hike is probably the best. It's located on a relatively quiet part of the lake, plus it has just enough distance associated with it to make it a pleasant outing, especially if you have young ones to introduce to hiking.

DIRECTIONS

Vista Point Recreation Area is 21 miles outside Raleigh on US 64 West, beyond Wilsonville. From Wilsonville, follow the brown signs to North Pea Ridge Road. Park at the first small parking area on your left as you drive in. Look for a crosswalk. From there you can see the trail board, tucked somewhat back into the pines.

DESCRIPTION

Named for its impressive view of Jordan Lake, Vista Point is a vital part of the Jordan Lake State Recreation Area. Jordan Lake, originally known as New Hope Lake, is a man-made lake created in the late 1960s. The recreation area encompasses 46,768 acres, of which 14,000 are the waters of Jordan Lake. As a spot for birding, diving ducks, loons, and gulls are on display in winter months. During warmer months, listen and look for common sparrows and pine warblers.

Like the other two Jordan Lake hikes, this trail winds around a mostly pine

KEY AT-A-GLANCE INFORMATION

Length:
2.7 miles

Configuration:
Loop

Difficulty:
Easy

Scenery:
Lake views

Exposure:
Shady

Solitude:
Probably won't be busy

Trail surface:
Pine needles, roots

Hiking time:
45 minutes

Access:
A $4 per car entrance fee is required during June, July, and August, and on weekends during April, May, and September.

Maps:
Available at the entrance gate

Facilities:
Rest rooms, water, picnic tables, camping

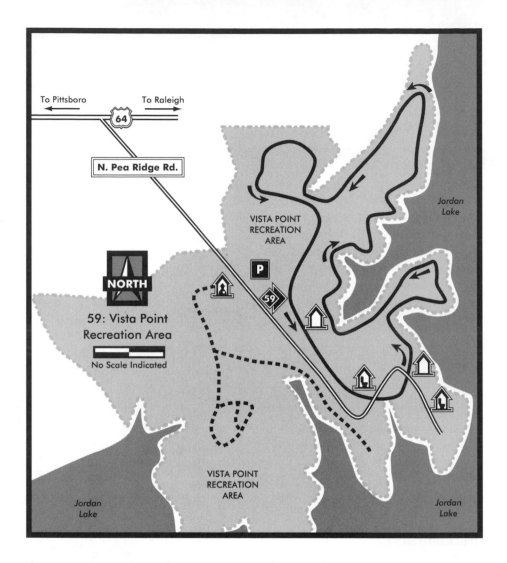

To Pittsboro

To Raleigh

64

N. Pea Ridge Rd.

Jordan Lake

VISTA POINT
RECREATION
AREA

P

NORTH

59

59: Vista Point
Recreation Area

No Scale Indicated

VISTA POINT
RECREATION
AREA

Jordan
Lake

Jordan
Lake

forest, in and around several coves. Be sure
to look for a tree about halfway into the
hike that resembles a slingshot. You'll be
amazed at how crooked the branches are!
Of special interest, I think, are the many
different varieties of mushrooms and toad-
stools. Whether it was because of recent
rainy days when I first hiked here or what,
the trail has lots of patches of tiny—I
mean tiny—mushrooms, in all kinds of
colors. The orange ones were brilliant, the
lavender ones quite pretty. Then there was
the rather large light purple with yellow

'shroom Ellen, Thresa, and I saw. (I might
also add we did yeoman's duty that morning taking out the spider webs!)

The trail becomes a bit confusing at
the lower parking lot; if you reach the
large picnic shelter that has a stone fireplace, you are off the trail! Whether you
retrace your steps to find the blazes or just
decide to walk across the parking lots to
return to your car doesn't really matter.
Either way, it's just yards up to the right.

There is one other trail at Vista Point.
The Tobacco Barn Trail is only a mile

184

Slingshot tree on the Vista Point Trail.

long and passes by, surprise, an old to-bacco barn.

To help you plan your trip, call Jordan Lake's automated weather information phone number at (919) 387-5969. The recording will give you the current temperature, wind direction, wind speed, and other information.

NEARBY ACTIVITIES

As with the other Jordan Lake hikes, it would be remiss not to visit the bald eagle observation deck at the north end of the lake. Although only a few pairs of bald eagles winter here, perhaps as many as three dozen migrate through the lake area each year. The observation deck, operated by the Audubon Society, is located off of NC 751. The best times to view the eagles are early morning and early evening. There is also a trail here; see the Wildlife Observation Trail on page 186 for details.

Wildlife Observation Trail

IN BRIEF

If your timing is right, that is, if you go early in the morning, you may be able to see bald eagles flying over Jordan Lake. Moreover, this self-guided trail has a most excellent brochure to explain what you're seeing along the way. Take the kids!

DIRECTIONS

This trail is located on NC 751 North, 5.8 miles from the intersection of US 64. Follow the brown binocular (wildlife viewing) signs.

When you reach the parking lot, look for the Wildlife Trail to begin far to the left of the marked trail that's easy to see. (This easy-to-see, unmarked web of foot-paths leads through the pine thicket to a fishing pond and is not a part of the Wildlife Trail. If you walk about 150 yards in, you'll see remnants of a baseball diamond, where the poison ivy and hon-eysuckle vines are slowing taking over what use to be the backstop.)

Look out for cyclists on this road, too! It is an enormously popular route with the two-wheeled set.

DESCRIPTION

This hike, a joint project of the New Hope Audubon Society, NC Wildlife Resources Commission's Nongame Program, and the U.S. Army Corp of Engineers, gets my vote as one of the best in the area. Much of the area Jordan Lake covers was once farmland. As you

KEY AT-A-GLANCE INFORMATION

Length:
1.5 miles

Configuration:
Loop

Difficulty:
Easy

Scenery:
Recovering young forest, Jordan Lake, raptors

Exposure:
Mostly shady

Solitude:
Busy early mornings

Trail surface:
Sand, roots

Hiking time:
40 minutes

Access:
No fees or permits

Maps:
None available; memorize the sign before you leave the parking area.

Facilities:
None

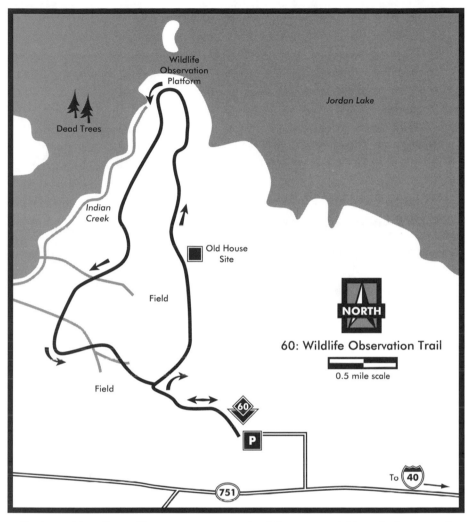

Wildlife
Observation
Platform

Jordan Lake

Dead Trees

Indian
Creek

Old House
Site

Field

NORTH

60: Wildlife Observation Trail

0.5 mile scale

Field

60

P

To 40

751

walk along this trail, you'll see remnants of farming: humpy tobacco rows not yet flattened—after 20-plus years!—remains of an old farmhouse, "conservation pines" planted to stop erosion, and, best of all, a platform that juts out into Jordan Lake to view bald eagles and ospreys. A board you'll pass on the way to the platform shows the various wing profiles of the raptors so that you'll have a better opportunity to identify them.

On my last hike out there, which admittedly was too late in the day for good birding, I read that the early morn-ing hikers spotted 11 eagles between 6 and 7:30 a.m.

It's interesting to note that this hike, along with the one at Hemlock Bluffs, provides some of the coolest summertime hiking. You should see plenty of wildflowers and butterflies in the fields along the trail. And the wind coming off Jordan Lake can't be beaten!

On the way back, check the trail carefully between interpretive Posts 6 and 7. The trail becomes very vague here, but with a little searching you'll find the correct path. (It's to the left, but not the

Watch for eagles from the wildlife observation platform on Jordan Lake.

left-most trail.) Continue to keep your eyes open; the same thing applies between Posts 9 and 10.

The adult bald eagle is fairly easy to recognize. It's characterized by its white head and tail, but does not show the distinctive marks, though, until the age of three or four years. The osprey, in contrast, has a white underbelly without the distinct white head and tail. Turkey vultures are very dark and have a much smaller head than the eagles. Take along an identification chart to help you distinguish further between eagles, turkey vultures, ospreys, and hawks.

Maintained by the New Hope Audubon Society in Chapel Hill, this hike and

viewing area are geared to promote the conservation of birds and protect the ecosystems in which they live. Interestingly, bald eagles were not observed on Jordan Lake until 1985. They have been closely watched since by the New Hope group.

To view the sometimes elusive eagles requires patience. The secret, notes the group's Web site is to "take your time and scan likely areas frequently. Eagles often sit and watch the area below them for food. Every hour or so, the eagle will break its inactivity with a reconnaissance flight." Try taking a picnic lunch and a pair of binoculars for a leisurely eagle spotting session.

Appendices

What good is hiking without the chance to break in boots, try out a new kind of sock, or see how the latest piece of outdoor wicky-wacky works? If you're looking for gear, here's where to go:

- Outdoor Provision Center with locations in Cary at the Cary Towne Center, (919) 380-0056; and in Raleigh at Crabtree Valley Mall (919) 781-1533; and Cameron Village (919) 833-1741.

- REI, located in Cary at Crossroads Plaza (919) 233-8444.

- Trail Shop in Chapel Hill on Franklin Street (919) 929-7626.

- Townsend Bertram and Company Adventure Outfitters in Carr Mill in Carrboro (919) 933-9712.

Appendix B: Places to Buy Maps

For Raleigh Bike Maps:

- All-Star Bike Shop located in Raleigh at Ridge Road Shopping Center, (919) 833-5070; and at Quail Corners shopping center on Falls of Neuse Road, (919) 876-9876. In Cary, you can find the All-Start Bike Shop at 740, East Chatham Street, (919) 469-1849.

- Spin Cycle, located in Cary at Saltbox Village on Kildaire Farm Road, (919) 460-9373.

- Town and Country Bicycle Shop at 12283 Capital Boulevard in Wake Forest, (919) 544-BIKE.

For City Greenway Maps:

- In Raleigh, at the Sertoma Arts Center, near Shelley Lake, (919) 420-2329.

- In Chapel Hill at the Community Center Park, (919) 968-2784

- In Durham at Durham Parks and Recreation, (919) 560-4355.

Index

About the Author

Lynn Setzer, a freelance writer living in Raleigh, hikes every chance she gets and is eager to share her love of the outdoors with you.

She comes by her hiking passion honestly. After spending too much time in office cubicles and breathing office air, she started hitting the trail as a way to find balance in her life. "I think better when I put one foot after the other," she declares.

"When work conspires to keep me from traveling to the wonderful Appalachian mountains, I find that I can hit one of the local trails for an hour or two or three and come back feeling refreshed."

If you see Lynn out in the woods, stop and say hello. In addition to her hiking regalia, she'll be wearing a Durham Bulls ball cap and a silly grin.